Daily Harvest

BAKERY & DELI COOKBOOK

Daily Harvest

BAKERY & DELI COOKBOOK

TERESA GORDON

PELICAN PUBLISHING COMPANY
GRETNA 2008

*To my husband, Johnny Gordon, who has supported me in
every project I have attempted even when some of those projects
were a little crazy. Johnny has always been by my side.*

*The word "Pelican" and the depiction of a pelican are trademarks
of Pelican Publishing Company, Inc., and are registered in the
U.S. Patent and Trademark Office.*

Library of Congress Cataloging-in-Publication Data

Gordon, Teresa.
  Daily Harvest Bakery & Deli cookbook / Teresa Gordon.
      p. cm.
  Includes index.
   ISBN-13: 978-1-58980-606-1 (hardcover : alk. paper)   1.   Baking. 2.
Cookery. 3. Daily Harvest Bakery & Deli. I. Title: Daily Harvest Bakery
and Deli cookbook. II. Title.
  TX765.G668 2008
  641.8'15 — dc22

                                          2008015251

Printed in China
Published by Pelican Publishing Company, Inc.
1000 Burmaster Street, Gretna, Louisiana 70053

Contents

Acknowledgments

First, I would like to thank the people who make the bakery and deli a huge success — my employees and customers. Without a caring staff, quality products, and faithful clients, I would be at my house watching soap operas. Now that would not be good, because I would be calling my husband, Johnny Gordon, every hour on the hour telling him how bored I was, and he would eventually sin by lying and saying he was having dropped calls on his cell phone. So, you all are great for my marriage, as well as Daily Harvest.

Second, I would like to thank my mama, Odeal Smith, who taught me little about cooking but a lot about life. My parents were in ministry, which means I'm a preacher's kid, and I have testimonies that I could share, but won't, that would reveal I've lived up to that title. As a child growing up, my mama said I could worry the horns right off a billy goat, and that was okay because she *truly* believed that if you spare the rod, you spoil the child. Believe me when I say my brother Rickey and I were not spoiled! We must have tried to act spoiled because she sure did use the rod on us. Somehow she always convinced us that it was for our own good, and it hurt her more than it did us. After my brother and I became adults, we laughed and picked at her about our stern upbringing and tried to get her to admit she really enjoyed spanking us. She never really answered us on that one.

I have seen my mama survive hardships that most of us could not have endured. Her faith in God has always been strong. She taught me to pray and when nothing happens, how to keep praying. She trained me to always treat people with respect and to make the best of a bad situation. She instilled the belief in me that if you want something and you don't get it, well, you just didn't want it bad enough.

About twelve years ago, my mama was stricken with the life-draining disease Alzheimer's and is now in stage four, the final stage. It breaks my heart to know that she will never read this cookbook. But I would still like to say, "Thank you, Mama. Just look at what you and God helped this aggravating preacher's kid accomplish."

Daily Harvest

BAKERY & DELI COOKBOOK

The Humble and Scary Beginnings of Daily Harvest

I don't know if you have ever experienced empty nest syndrome or not, but I believe the emptying of my nest was one of the forces that kicked off my desire to open Daily Harvest Bakery & Deli. When my daughter, Katina, married Josh, my handsome son-in-law, and my son, Justin, graduated from high school, I felt I had nothing to occupy my time. My husband is a mechanical contractor and his business is very time consuming. For some reason, he felt he didn't have time for my twenty-five phone calls per day.

One day while watching TV, I tuned to the *700 Club,* and they were featuring a story about a woman in Atlanta, Georgia, who was grinding grain and making Ezekiel bread. For some reason her personal story and the process of how she baked the bread fascinated me. I had never baked bread; as a matter of fact, I had never cooked much at all. My children will tell you that I raised them on hot dogs and TV dinners.

I called Johnny (phone call number twenty-six that day) and told him the whole story. He told me I could order some of the bread, but I explained to him that I didn't want to *buy* the bread. I wanted to learn how to *bake* it. I wanted to go to Atlanta to check out this Ezekiel-bread-baking lady. So that weekend we took a road trip to Atlanta, and it was then I decided to become a baker.

I discovered that you needed grain and a mill to grind the grain. We bought a small mill that would grind about two cups at a time and a twenty-five-pound bag of grain. I thought we would still have some grain left over when the Lord returned. I began making bread; I was so proud of myself. I think Johnny was afraid to try it, but in order to make me happy, he ate a slice. I think he was shocked when he liked it.

After the successful husband-wasn't-poisoned-and-didn't-die test, I began baking bread for my friends and family. One day my son's girlfriend, Sarah, took some loaves home, and her mother, Gale, sampled them. Gale called me on the phone and asked me to tell her how I made this bread.

Now, you have to understand, I have never been a person who lacked for words, so it was easy for me to share with Gale everything about this new adventure. I started with, "Well, there I was in my living room, sitting on my sofa, scanning through the TV channels, when I saw a lady making bread with ingredients like pinto beans, spelt, rye, and green lentils." (At that time, I didn't even know what a green lentil was.) I told her all about our trip to Atlanta, Georgia. I explained how we travelled to another town to purchase the necessary tools and ingredients.

Suddenly, my kitchen looked like a grain elevator with beans scattered all around, and for the first time in my life, I was baking bread! Not only baking bread, I was baking this weird bread called Ezekiel bread.

Okay, I must confess that I had made bread and rolls before, and it wasn't hard to make, but when I hit that paper can on the corner of my kitchen counter it sure did scare me. You know what I mean—the first time you hit it you do it kind of soft, but it doesn't open. So you hit it a little harder, then even harder. By the time that crazy can popped open, every muscle in my body was tense.

As I continued my story, Gale would jump in and say, "Uh," or "Oh, my!" I told her how good the Ezekiel bread tasted and how this had birthed in me a concern for my health and the health of my family members as well as a newly found desire for baking.

At that time, Gale was working for a local attorney, but she offered to help me. Not long after that talk, at a local beauty salon, we sold our first loaf of bread. Requests for my bread began pouring in, and I had a hard time keeping up with the orders.

I wanted to open a bakery, but I was afraid. I had not worked at a job since I was in high school. Gale offered to quit her job and help me, and I thought this girl must be as crazy as I am, but I was greatly encouraged by her offer. I needed someone to believe in my dream enough to go out on the limb with me. Gale did. We decided to go into business.

Starting the business was not easy; we didn't have any idea what we were doing. I had no experience in baking or business, and the only experience Gale had was cooking for her five children. I often became discouraged, wondering to myself, "What was I thinking when I made this decision?" But, I would reflect on something my mama taught me, "Every road has a turn in it; so when you get discouraged, don't stop because, before long, the road will make a turn in your favor." I knew I wanted Daily Harvest Bakery & Deli to be a success; therefore, I refused to let disappointments, failures, and difficulties get me down.

I began researching whole grains and its health benefits, healthy sweeteners, chemical free products, fruits, and vegetables, and on April 6, 2004, we opened our doors. We started our workday at 3:00 A.M. Gale ran the office and baked cookies, and I ground the grain and baked bread. I didn't know if anyone would show up or not. Then one by one the people came, and came, and came, and they're still coming.

Throughout this process, the blessings have outweighed the hardships, and it seems that people like our products and want to know more about us. Since the opening, we have been featured in *Southern Living* magazine and won the Northeast Louisiana Small Business Award in 2006. That same year we opened a second Daily Harvest Bakery & Deli, in West Monroe, and in January of 2007, we were voted Best Bakery in *Road Trip! Magazine.* I have been a guest speaker at local universities and churches, sharing our story and our philosophy. I can be seen every Friday morning on a local TV station doing the cooking segment, and you can listen to me on a local radio station many times throughout the day, discussing our menu and daily specials. Wow! I would never have dreamed all these things could happen to me. The old adage, "You've come a long way, baby," really applies to Daily Harvest because here we are four years later, two small-town girls—me a native of Jonesboro-Hodge, Louisiana, and Gale a native of Oak Grove,

Louisiana—still going strong. Gale still runs the office, and I deal more in the marketing and public relations departments.

In this book, I would like to share with you a mini-version of the Daily Harvest Bakery & Deli's story, as well as many of the recipes that have made us successful. As I said, we've had some setbacks and disappointments along the way, but we have also been blessed with some great accomplishments. If you have a dream in your heart that you would love to pursue but you are afraid to begin, the story of our humble and scary beginnings should encourage you to step out and follow that dream. I have only one word of advice—make sure you stay focused and when disappointments come, and they will, dig in your heals and don't give up. Like the Bible says, "Cast thy bread upon the waters: for thou shalt find it after many days. . . . In the morning sow thy seed, and in the evening withhold not thine hand: for thou knowest not whether shall prosper, either this or that, or whether they both shall be alike good" (Ecclesiastes 11:1, 6).

And to think, it all began with one loaf of Ezekiel bread!

Gale Green

I would like to say thank you to Daily Harvest. You may ask how that is possible since Daily Harvest is a business and has no ears to hear. But I disagree; everyone who reads this cookbook becomes the eyes and ears of Daily Harvest. It is more than a place, more than produce; it is an experience. Daily Harvest is so much more to me than just a business or a place to work; it is an entity full of opportunities. No one appreciates it more than me because Daily Harvest has been monumental in my life for several reasons. It came at an extremely pivotal point in my life. The business gave me direction and a place to put my focus. It gave me purpose at a time in my life when purpose would have been hard to find. I had

to have a reason to get up every morning, and because of Daily Harvest, I continue to do so.

Daily Harvest has opened a completely new world to me, a world of people, places, and pleasures. I have met so many wonderful people across the counter at Daily Harvest. We are fortunate to have a wonderful pool of customers. It has been remarkable to hear the stories they tell, and I have gleaned information that I would have otherwise never heard. I recognize faces everywhere I go, and it is a wonderful feeling to have someone greet me in the mall or the grocery store and follow up with "We love Daily Harvest." It gives me a warm feeling and puts a smile on my face to know we are touching people. I have formed bonds with a select handful of people that will remain long after the lights are turned off and the open sign goes dark. Naming them is not necessary because they know who they are.

Being a mother of five children, the majority of my time in the past was filled with going to church events, ball games, doctor offices, school productions, grocery stores, etc. Needless to say, there was very little time left for me and certainly fewer moments of free time. Since Daily Harvest came into my life, Teresa and I have had the opportunity to visit cities I would have never traveled to. Undoubtedly if you go anywhere with Teresa, there will also be some time for fun. We learned a lot, but we have also played a lot, and I have experienced hours of what I will just refer to as "life."

It has been a pleasure to work each day with one of the most talented, creative, and vibrant people I know. There have been few dull moments with Teresa Gordon in the house. Anyone who knows her, knows I am speaking the truth. My life has been action packed since the day I met her. We have worked hard, but the rewards have been worth every long hour spent here. We have had fun interacting with our favorite customers and our never-ending stream of employees as they come and go. We have laughed over things that have been said and done. Maybe one day we will share some of those candid moments with you, but for now, those belong to us, and on days when things are about to fall apart, one of us will say, "Hey, do you remember when . . ." After we stop laughing, we realize that whatever we are facing it too will pass. Laughter is good like medicine reads the Bible, and I guess God knew we would need much medicine because he has given us many opportunities to laugh.

Through good times and bad times, we have remained. It is my hope that Daily Harvest will be here until our wrinkles take over and our hair turns a whiter shade of gray.

In conclusion, I would like to encourage anyone with a dream to seek it out, pursue it, and allow it to grow into reality. It may be a long road with many curves, hills, and bumps, but it will be one worth taking. A trip to remember.

Thanks to Teresa Gordon and her dream; our many customers and their faithfulness; our employees who stayed when times got tough; my children for being understanding of the long hours necessary to make the business work; and thanks to the Lord for giving us strength. Because of all of these people, I have been given a chance to do things I would have never dreamed.

The Daily Harvest Workers

The workers at Daily Harvest Bakery & Deli are a key to our success. Like Chaucer's pilgrims in the *Canterbury Tales,* they came to us with unique personalities and life experiences. They are colorful, witty, hardworking, and interesting. Working in a bakery as fast-paced and intense as Daily Harvest is, is not an easy job. The hours are long, the work unrelenting, demanding a commitment and flexibility that does not come easily to most people. Gale and I are fortunate to keep one out of ten people we hire as long-term employees. Like Jesus said, "The harvest is plenteous, but the labourers are few" (Matthew 9:37). On the following pages, you will find pictures and descriptions of our committed workers.

Cortez Roberts

Cortez is no doubt the most colorful employee at Daily Harvest. He is a happy-go-lucky, fun-loving guy, and this attitude is reflected in his personality. He honestly loves Daily Harvest customers. He is not afraid to try anything. Even if he has no idea what he has to do, he will try it.

Cortez is fast, and you had better get out of his way or he will run you over. He even talks fast, sometimes too fast. I have seen customers squint their eyes and slightly turn their heads trying to understand Cortez explain a product. But, they don't care; they love Cortez as much as he loves them.

Cortez has been at Daily Harvest longer than any other employee has. He is very faithful and can cook and bake most everything on our menu. Sometimes I let Cortez carry breakfast to one of our local radio stations, and the DJs will talk to Cortez live on the radio. I will never forget the day he told the entire listening area that we might open a new Daily Harvest in Ruston, Louisiana, or Dallas, Texas. I have no idea where Cortez obtained this inside information. For two weeks, we had people from Ruston asking when and where our new bakery would be located.

Once he had concerns about my appearance so he offered his innocent, yet straightforward, advice. It was mid-February, and I found myself not well. I had aches and pains all over my body from a fever. I knew I had to work through it because Gale was out of town and we were short-handed. It was day three of my illness; my nose was red, my hair had gone flat due to lack of care, and my feet were dragging. I had been in the office all morning and decided to go to the front for something when Cortez stopped me and said, "Ms. Teresa, Mr. Wyman is here. I think you need to put on some make-up." I know Mr. Wyman is a regular and valuable customer, but was it courage or craziness that let those words come out of his mouth!

Mr. Wyman was at the front with a big smile on his face, waving.

At this point, I had to go and speak to him even though I looked just like I felt, but first, with my low nasal voice, I asked Cortez, "Have you lost your MIND? You should never tell a woman she needs on makeup." Then I gave him a forced smile, and as usual, Cortez gave that big ol' grin and said, "Oh, sorry, Ms. Teresa."

I said all of that to say I am very proud of Cortez. If you find yourself having a bad day and want a little "pick me up," come to Daily Harvest and see that big smile on Cortez's face; your worries will melt away.

Annette Lively

When Annette applied for a job here at Daily Harvest, I asked her if she had any experience in baking or cooking for a restaurant. Her answer was, "I watch the Food Network." I was a little worried, but I can tell you one thing, watching TV has been a good thing for Annette. She is a very hard worker, and we all know that a hard-working employee is hard to find. Annette knows her way around a kitchen. She can multi-task from the front door of the bakery and deli to the back. She can listen to my ideas and make them a reality, and I have had some *crazy* ideas.

Customer service comes naturally for Annette, and I believe she is one of the best baristas in north Louisiana. She listens to what a customer wants, and she puts her expertise to work. Her barista skills come easy to her because she loves to drink coffee.

Annette also likes to help with TV commercials. The only problem is that she likes to focus on the camera more than the product she is working on. We have laughed and picked at her because she will give her blinking-come-on eyes to the camera. She denies it, but we have a copy of the commercial for proof. We like to think of her as the siren of the bakery world. Oh, and by the way Annette is a great cook!

Loretta Bowman

Loretta is probably one of the most easygoing people I know, and she is an asset to Daily Harvest. Though she was not born and raised in the South, she has definitely taken on a Southern-girl mentality. She is good with our customers and her fellow employees. Loretta builds our wraps for the panini grill and works the sandwich station. She also helps with the items on our catering menu.

Cedric Harris

Cedric is the kind of employee every employer wishes she had. Cedric comes to work, does his job, and goes home. Cedric not only keeps our dishes washed and stocks groceries, he also is a good baker. If you enjoy eating cookies from Daily Harvest Bakery & Deli, it would be a good guess to say that you are eating a cookie that Cedric baked.

There have been times when someone did not show up for work, and I would call Cedric at 3:00 A.M. and say, "Cedric, I need your help." He would get on his bicycle and ride three miles across town to help me bake. Everyday before Cedric leaves, he asks, "Mrs. Teresa, is there anything else you need me to do?"

Now that's a good employee!

Amanda Hunter

Amanda is about 5 feet 2 inches in stature but do not let that fool you. She possesses a feisty spirit and is able and willing to handle any conflict or situation. However, I am very careful about what I ask her to do, such as, "Don't let the truck driver leave before we check our delivery," because she will gladly follow through with the task by whatever means necessary. She will do anything from barring the door to threats to physically holding the poor man against his will. Amanda is a steady and faithful employee and contributes to the success of Daily Harvest.

Misty Bussell

Misty is the kitchen manager at Daily Harvest Bakery & Deli. She is probably the most balanced manager I have ever seen. She knows how to work hard and still have fun. Although she is a little younger than me (OK a lot younger), we still think alike when it comes to work ethics. Misty is a young lady with a great future ahead of her. I am glad to have her on our Daily Harvest team.

Owen Ramsey

I guess you could say that Owen is a chef turned baker. He worked as the head chef of a local fine-dining restaurant for years before coming on board at Daily Harvest. I do not know if I have ever worked with anyone more cooperative than Owen. If I tell him we need ten extra muffins, he replies with a big ol' grin. If I say we need 110 muffins, he still replies with that same smile. I do not have the passive personality that Owen possesses, and though Gale disagrees, maybe in time it will rub off on me. Maybe?

Breads

When it comes to bread at Daily Harvest, we don't loaf around! Everything we bake has been a trial and error. I can testify to that because I was the first person in charge of baking bread, and if you will remember, I confessed that I had no idea what I was doing. The bread baking came about through much research, a lot of long hard hours, and, yes, even a few tears.

True, man does not live by bread alone, but if you eat the right kind of bread, you almost can. One feels a great sense of satisfaction from making one's own bread. I was baking bread so much that my oven stayed on practically day and night. I'll put it to you like this: My husband, Johnny, was getting more than his share of fiber intake per day (don't tell him I said that). I think he was ready for me to open the business so he wouldn't have to eat bread for breakfast, mid-morning snack, lunch, mid-afternoon snack, and you guessed it, supper.

Once you successfully bake your first nutritious loaf, you will have a hard time returning to the fluffy, light, tasteless bread on the grocery stores' shelves. Fresh stone-ground whole-wheat bread is definitely the bread you should choose for you and your family, but I would not suggest serving it eight times per day.

First, we'll start with a basic recipe, and then we'll reveal several recipes that will motivate you to become your family's baker and a well-bread person. I will also share some tips that I have discovered since my bread-baking days began. Perhaps this will give you a small head start on yours.

Teresa's Tips for Baking Bread

For best results with bread, the water temperature should be very warm, between 110 and 120 degrees F, but no hotter.

If you suspect your yeast may be expired, test a teaspoon of yeast in a cup of warm water (110 degrees F). Add in a pinch of sugar or honey. If your mix bubbles within 10 minutes, it should be active enough to make your dough rise.

Always preheat your oven.

If you want a softer crust on your bread, butter the tops when removing it from the oven.

If your bread "flops," don't throw it away. It can be used for your bread pudding, to make croutons, or with several other recipes in this cookbook. For bread pudding, you can grind it and store it in the freezer in a Ziploc bag until ready to use.

Once your bread has been removed from the oven, it should cool on a wire rack.

If you have dough left over, it can be wrapped very tightly in freezer wrap and kept in your refrigerator for several days. Let it come to room temperature when ready to use.

When making bread, always have the flour at room temperature before adding it to your mixer. Warm flour encourages your bread to rise nice and high. (This is for those of you who mill your flour ahead and keep it stored in the freezer.) And when allowing your dough to rise, keep it in a warm place.

Baked bread should be stored airtight in a cool place. Do not refrigerate, as the condensation promotes mold. Since there are no added preservatives, Daily Harvest bread has a 4 to 5 day shelf life.

Stone-Ground Whole-Wheat Bread

2 cups hot water, about 110 degrees
½ cup olive oil
½ cup honey or agave*
5 cups freshly milled whole-wheat flour
3½ tsp. instant yeast
2 tsp. sea salt
½ tsp. dough enhancer, optional
½ tsp. gluten

Combine water, oil, and honey. Add 3 cups of freshly milled whole-wheat flour, yeast, sea salt, dough enhancer, and gluten. Mix well with a wire whisk. Let stand until it begins to bubble, about 20 to 30 minutes.

Add the remaining 2 cups of flour and knead until smooth and elastic, about 10 minutes. If your dough is still sticky to the touch, add a little more flour until it looses its sticky texture. Let this rise again until it doubles in size. Shape into 2 loaves and place in greased bread pans. Let this rise again. Bake in 350-degree oven for about 30 minutes.

Yields: 2 loaves

*If you prefer bread with a less sweet taste, cut the honey in ½.

Cheddar-Herb Loaf

2 cups warm water, 110-115 degrees
½ cup olive oil
½ cup honey or agave nectar*
5-7 cups freshly milled whole-wheat flour
3½ tsp. instant yeast
2 tsp. sea salt
½ tsp. dough enhancer, optional
½ tsp. gluten
2 cups shredded cheddar cheese
½ tsp. dried parsley
⅛ tsp. garlic powder
⅛ tsp. paprika
¼ tsp. Parmesan cheese

GARLIC BUTTER:
½ stick butter, melted
½ tsp. garlic salt

Combine water, oil, and honey. Add 2 cups of freshly milled whole-wheat flour, yeast, sea salt, dough enhancer, and gluten. Mix well with wire whisk. Let stand until it begins to bubble.

Meanwhile, combine cheddar cheese, parsley, garlic powder, paprika, and Parmesan cheese. Mix well and set aside.

Add flour until the dough forms a smooth elastic ball and

knead, about 5 minutes. Roll dough into a large rectangular shape $1/4$ inch thick. Sprinkle the cheese mixture on $1/2$ of the rectangle. Roll into a cylinder shape and pinch edges to seal. Form into a circle. Place in a greased 9-inch-round cake pan. Let rise until it doubles in size. Brush the top with the garlic butter and sprinkle with Parmesan cheese. Bake at 350 degrees for about 30 minutes.

*If you prefer bread with a less sweet taste, cut the honey in $1/2$.

Cinnamon-Raisin Walnut Bread

2 cups warm water, 110-115 degrees
$1/2$ cup olive oil
$1/2$ cup honey or agave nectar*
5-7 cups freshly milled whole-wheat flour
$3 1/2$ tsp. instant yeast
2 tsp. sea salt
$1/2$ tsp. dough enhancer, optional
$1/2$ tsp. gluten
1 cup dried raisins
1 cup chopped walnut pieces
$1/2$ tbsp. cinnamon

Combine water, oil, and honey. Add 2 cups of freshly milled whole-wheat flour, yeast, sea salt, dough enhancer, and gluten. Mix well with wire whisk. Let stand until it begins to bubble.

Add flour until the dough forms a smooth elastic ball and knead, about 5 minutes. During the kneading process, add the raisins, walnuts, and cinnamon.

Place dough in a large greased bowl and let it rise until it doubles in size. Shape into 2 loaves and place in greased bread pans. Let this rise to the top of the pan. Bake at 350 degrees for about 30 minutes.

Yields: 2 loaves

*If you prefer bread with a less sweet taste, cut the honey in $1/2$.

Cinnamon-Swirl Bread

2 cups warm water, 110-115 degrees
½ cup olive oil
2 eggs
½ cup honey or agave nectar*
5-7 cups freshly milled whole-wheat flour
3½ tsp. instant yeast
2 tsp. sea salt
½ tsp. dough enhancer, optional
½ tsp. gluten
¼ cup melted butter
2 tbsp. cinnamon
½ cup sucanat with honey

Combine water, oil, eggs, and honey. Add 2 cups of freshly milled whole-wheat flour, yeast, sea salt, dough enhancer, and gluten. Mix well with wire whisk. Let stand until it begins to bubble.

Add flour until the dough forms a smooth elastic ball and knead, about 5 minutes. Place in well-greased bowl. Let rise and then turn onto a floured surface. Roll out into a rectangle shape about ½ inch thick. Spread evenly with melted butter, sprinkle with cinnamon and sucanat with honey. Roll into a shape to fit your loaf pans. Brush on more melted butter. Bake at 350 degrees for about 30 to 35 minutes.

Yields: 2 loaves

*If you prefer bread with a less sweet taste, cut the honey in ½.

Cranberry-Pecan Bread

2 cups warm water, 110-115 degrees
½ cup olive oil
½ cup honey or agave nectar*
5-7 cups freshly milled whole-wheat flour
3½ tsp. instant yeast
2 tsp. sea salt
½ tsp. dough enhancer, optional
½ tsp. gluten
1 cup dried cranberries
1 cup chopped pecan pieces

Combine water, oil, and honey. Add 2 cups of freshly milled whole-wheat flour, yeast, sea salt, dough enhancer, and gluten. Mix well with wire whisk. Let stand until it begins to bubble.

Add flour until the dough forms a smooth elastic ball and knead, about 5 minutes. During the kneading process, add the cranberries and pecans.

Place dough in a large greased bowl and let it rise until it doubles in size. Shape into loaves and place in greased bread pans. Let this rise to the top of the pan. Bake at 350 degrees for about 30 minutes.

Yields: 2 loaves

*If you prefer bread with less a sweet taste, cut the honey in ½.

French Bread

6 cups stone-ground whole-wheat flour
2½ tbsp. active dry yeast
2½ tbsp. sea salt
2 cups warm water, 110 degrees F
1 tbsp. cornmeal
1 egg white
1 tbsp. water

In a large bowl, combine 2 cups whole-wheat flour, yeast, and salt. Stir in 2 cups warm water and beat until well blended using a stand mixer with a dough-hook attachment. Using a wooden spoon, stir in as much of the remaining flour as you can.

On a lightly floured surface, knead in enough flour to make a stiff dough that is smooth and elastic. Knead for about 8 to 10 minutes total. Shape into a ball. Place dough in a greased bowl and turn once. Cover. Let rise in a warm place until doubled. Punch dough down and divide in ½. Turn out onto a lightly floured surface. Cover. Let rest for 10 minutes. Roll each ½ into a large rectangle. Roll up, starting from the long side. Moisten edge with water and seal. Taper ends.

Grease a large baking sheet. Sprinkle with cornmeal. Place loaves, seam side down, on the prepared baking sheet. Lightly beat the egg white with 1 tbsp. of water and brush on. Cover with a damp cloth. Let rise until nearly doubled, 35 to 40 minutes.

With a very sharp knife, make 3 or 4 diagonal cuts about ¼ inch deep across top of each loaf. Bake in a preheated 375-degree oven for 20 minutes. Brush again with egg-white mixture. Bake for an additional 15 to 20 minutes, or until bread tests done*. If necessary, cover loosely with foil to prevent overbrowning. Remove from baking sheet and cool on a wire rack.

*When the bread is done, it makes a hollow sound when thumped. If bread begins to draw up from the sides while cooling, it is not done.

Focaccia Bread

2 cups warm water, 110-115 degrees
½ cup olive oil
½ cup honey or agave nectar*
5-7 cups stone-ground whole-wheat flour
3½ tsp. instant yeast
2 tsp. sea salt
½ tsp. dough enhancer, optional
½ tsp. gluten
½ tsp. dried basil
1 tsp. dried oregano
1 tsp. garlic powder
1 tbsp. grated Parmesan cheese
2 tbsp. olive oil

Combine water, oil and honey. Add 2 cups of whole-wheat flour, yeast, sea salt, dough enhancer, and gluten. Mix well with wire whisk. Let stand until it begins to bubble.

Meanwhile, mix in a bowl basil, oregano, garlic powder, Parmesan, and olive oil. Set aside.

To the dough, add flour until the dough forms a smooth elastic ball and knead, about 5 minutes. Place dough in a large greased bowl and let it rise until it doubles in size. Punch down and roll into a flat ½-inch rectangle shape. Pat out onto a greased baking sheet. Top with the seasoning. Bake at 375 degrees for about 15 to 20 minutes.

*If you prefer bread with a less sweet taste, cut the honey in ½.

Jalapeño-Cheese Bread

2 cups warm water, 110 degrees
3½ tsp. yeast
½ cup honey or agave nectar
½ cup olive oil
2 tsp. sea salt
½ tsp. dough enhancer, optional
½ tsp. gluten
5-7 cups stone-ground whole-wheat flour
½ cup chopped jalapeños
1 cup grated cheddar cheese

Measure all ingredients in a mixing bowl, except jalapeños and cheese, and mix well with wire whisk. Let this mixture stand until bubbly. At least 15 minutes, but not longer than 30 minutes.

After the time has elapsed, using a mixer on low speed, begin adding more freshly milled flour until sides of bowl begin to clean. Switch to a higher speed as dough becomes stiffer. Begin kneading when sides are just about clean. Knead for 6 minutes. Add jalapeños and cheese. Continue to knead for 2 minutes. Place dough on oiled surface. Weigh out in 1-lb. portions. Let rise in proofer or warm place until dough is to the top of the pan. Bake at 350 degrees for 30 to 40 minutes. Remove from pans and cool on wire rack.

Yields: 2 loaves

Onion-Cheese Loaf

2 cups warm water, 110-115 degrees
½ cup olive oil
½ cup honey or agave nectar*
2 eggs
5-7 cups stone-ground whole-wheat flour
3½ tsp. instant yeast
2 tsp. sea salt
½ tsp. dough enhancer, optional
½ tsp. gluten
1 cup diced yellow onions
1 cup grated cheddar cheese

Combine water, oil, honey, and eggs. Add 2 cups of whole-wheat flour, yeast, sea salt, dough enhancer, and gluten. Mix well with wire whisk. Let stand until it begins to bubble.

Add flour until the dough forms a smooth elastic ball and knead, about 5 minutes. During the kneading process, add the diced onions and cheddar cheese.

Place dough in a large greased bowl and let it rise until it doubles in size. Shape into loaves and place in greased bread pans. Let this rise to the top of the pan. Bake at 350 degrees for about 30 minutes.

Yields 2 loaves

*If you prefer bread with a less sweet taste, cut the honey in ½.

Pita Bread

2 tsp. dry yeast
1¼ cups warm water, about 110-115 degrees
1 tbsp. sucanat with honey
3½ cups stone-ground whole-wheat flour
½ tsp. sea salt

Add yeast to ¼ cup of the water. Add sucanat with honey and let stand for 10 minutes.

To a warm bowl, add 2½ cups stone-ground whole-wheat flour and sea salt. Form a well in the center and pour in yeast mixture and remaining warm water. Begin to mix with hand, wooden spoon, or dough hook, adding remaining flour as needed. Turn out onto a floured surface and knead for 10 to 15 minutes, or until smooth and no longer sticky. Oil a large bowl, place dough in bowl. Cover with a damp cloth and set in a warm place for 1½ hours. Dough should double in size.

Once dough has risen, knead for a few minutes and then divide into balls about 2½ inches in diameter. Roll balls into circles on a lightly floured surface with rolling pin. The circles should be about ¼ inch thick. Preheat oven to 475 degrees. Place loaves on a greased baking sheet and bake for 5 minutes, or until a golden brown. Place on wire rack for cooling.

Yields: 6 loaves

Oat Loaf

2 cups warm water, 110-115 degrees
½ cup olive oil
½ cup honey or agave nectar*
5-7 cups freshly milled whole-wheat flour, red wheat if
    available
3½ tsp. instant yeast
2 tsp. sea salt
½ tsp. dough enhancer, optional
½ tsp. gluten
1 cup organic rolled oats

Combine water, oil, and honey. Add 2 cups of freshly milled whole-wheat flour, yeast, sea salt, dough enhancer, and gluten. Mix well with wire whisk. Let stand until it begins to bubble.

Once it bubbles, add flour until the dough forms a smooth elastic ball and knead, about 5 minutes. Add the rolled oats while in the kneading process. Place dough in a large greased bowl and let it rise until it doubles in size. Shape into loaves and place in greased bread pan. Let this rise to the top of the pan. Bake at 350 degrees for about 30 minutes.

Yields: 2 loaves

*If you prefer bread with a less sweet taste, cut the honey in ½.

Roasted Garlic and Rosemary Braid

ROASTED GARLIC:
3 heads garlic

GARLIC BUTTER:
½ cup melted butter
½ tsp. garlic salt

BREAD DOUGH:
5-7 cups stone-ground whole-wheat flour
2 cups warm water, 110 degrees
3½ tsp. yeast
½ cup honey or agave nectar
½ cup olive oil
2 tsp. sea salt
½ tsp. dough enhancer, optional
½ tsp. gluten

For roasted garlic: Remove papery outer skin from garlic, but do not separate cloves. Cut off top of garlic heads, leaving the root end intact. Place cut side up in baking pan. Brush tops with olive oil and sprinkle with dried rosemary. Cover pan with foil and bake at 425 degrees for 30 to 35 minutes or until soft. Remove from oven and cool for 10 to 15 minutes. Squeeze softened garlic into bowl, add water and lightly mash. Set aside.

For garlic butter: In a bowl, mix butter and garlic salt. Set aside.

For dough: Beginning with 5 cups of flour, measure all ingredients in bowl and mix well with wire whisk. Let this mixture stand until bubbly, at least 15 minutes, but no longer than 30 minutes. After time has elapsed, add roasted garlic paste. In a mixer, on low speed, begin adding more freshly milled flour until sides of bowl begin to clean. Change mixer to higher speed as dough becomes stiffer. Begin kneading when sides are just about clean. Dough should not be sticky. Knead for 8 minutes. Place dough on oiled surface. Weigh out in 1-lb. portions. Divide each portion into 3 equal-size balls. Roll each ball into a rope about 11 inches long. Lay all 3 ropes side by side. Turn under on the top end. Braid. When at the end, pinch all 3 ends together and turn under. Let rise in proofer. Bake at 350 degrees for 30 to 40 minutes. Brush with garlic butter as soon as bread is removed from oven. Remove from pan and cool on wire rack.

Sesame-Seed Loaf

2 cups warm water, 110-115 degrees
½ cup olive oil
½ cup honey or agave nectar*
5-7 cups stone-ground whole-wheat flour
3½ tsp. instant yeast
2 tsp. sea salt
½ tsp. dough enhancer, optional
½ tsp. gluten
½ cup sesame seeds
Melted butter

Combine water, oil, and honey. Add 2 cups of freshly milled whole-wheat flour, yeast, sea salt, dough enhancer, and gluten. Mix well with wire whisk. Let stand until it begins to bubble.

Once it bubbles, add flour until the dough forms a smooth elastic ball and knead, about 5 minutes. Knead in the sesame seeds at this point. Place dough in a large greased bowl and let it rise until it doubles in size. Shape into loaves and place in greased bread pans. Let this rise to the top of the pan. Mop on a little melted butter and sprinkle with sesame seeds. Bake at 350 degrees for about 30 minutes.

Yields: 2 loaves

*If you prefer bread with a less sweet taste, cut the honey in ½.

Veggie Loaf

2½ tsp. active dry yeast
¾ cup fresh-squeezed tomato juice
1 tbsp. warm water
¼ tsp. ground ginger
¼ tsp. sucanat with honey
1¾ cup stone-ground whole-wheat flour
2 tbsp. wheat germ
¼ tsp. sea salt
½ cup grated carrots
½ cup thinly sliced celery
½ cup diced red bell pepper
½ cup finely chopped onions
¼ cup chopped green parsley
1 tbsp. olive oil

Dissolve yeast in warm tomato juice and warm water.

In a bowl, combine ginger, sucanat, whole-wheat flour, wheat germ, sea salt, carrots, celery, red bell pepper, onions, parsley, and oil. Stir in the yeast mixture and knead to form a soft dough. Sit in warm place and allow to double in size. Punch down and place into a greased loaf pan. Allow to rise again. Bake at 350 degrees for 20 minutes.

Whole-Wheat Pizza Crust

1 cup warm water, 95-115 degrees
2 tbsp. honey or agave nectar
½ tsp. sea salt
2 tbsp. yeast*
3½ stone-ground whole-wheat flour
¼ cup olive oil

Pour warm water into a bowl. The water should be about 95 to 115 degrees. Test it with your hand. It should feel very warm, but comfortable. Add the honey and salt. Mix on low until well blended. Add the yeast and mix. Let this mixture sit for about 5 minutes. Add 1 cup of whole-wheat flour and the olive oil and mix until well blended. Add the rest of the flour and mix well. The dough should turn into a ball. If the dough does not ball up, it's too dry; add water 1 tbsp. at a time until it does. If your mixture is more like a batter, add flour 1 tbsp. at a time. Adding water or flour as needed to get the right consistency will assure you always get a perfect dough. Just remember to do it in small amounts.

Once the dough has formed a ball, place the ball on a floured board and knead for about a minute. This builds the gluten, which helps the dough to rise and become fluffy when cooked. Place the dough in a plastic grocery bag or a covered bowl and store in a warm, dry area to rise.

After about 45 minutes, the dough should have doubled in size. Punch it down. Let it rise for another 1 to 1½ hours. The dough is now ready to be rolled out. You can punch the dough down one more time if you like and wait another 1 or 2 hours before rolling out. The choice is yours.

When you are ready to bake the dough, bake in a 350-degree-oven for 10 minutes.

*I like my dough a little yeasty, but you can use less.

Banana Nut Bread

½ **cup butter**
½ **cup honey or agave nectar**
2 **eggs**
1 **tsp. vanilla**
2 **cups stone-ground whole-wheat flour**
1 **tsp. baking soda**
½ **tsp. salt**
4 **bananas, mashed**
1 **cup chopped pecans**

In a bowl, cream the butter, honey, eggs, and vanilla. Add to the mixture, flour, baking soda, salt, bananas, and pecans. Mix well and pour into small bread loaf pans. Sprinkle the top of each loaf with a few chopped pecans. Bake at 325 for 45 minutes.

Yields: 3 loaves

Jalapeño Cornbread

½ lb. butter, melted
4 eggs
1 can cream-style corn
¼ cup chopped onions
¼ cup chopped jalapenos
¾ cup sucanat with honey
1 cup fresh-ground cornmeal
1 cup stone-ground whole-wheat flour
1¼ tbsp. baking powder
½ tsp. sea salt
1 cup shredded cheddar cheese

Combine the first 6 ingredients in a large bowl. Mix well. Add to this the remaining ingredients and cheese. Mix well. Pour into a 13-x-9 baking dish or into individual loaf pans, which is how we bake it at Daily Harvest. Bake for 20 to 25 minutes at 350 degrees.

Caramel-Apple Flatbread

2¼ cups stone-ground whole-wheat flour
½ cup oats
1 tbsp. sucanat with honey
2¼ tsp. quick rising yeast
½ tsp. cinnamon
½ tsp. sea salt
¾ cup water
1 tbsp. olive oil
1 egg white
1 cup unpeeled chopped apple

TOPPING:
¾ cup oats
⅔ cup sucanat, brown sugar can be substituted
½ tsp. cinnamon
¾ cup low-fat sour cream
¼ cup chopped pecans and/or walnuts

Lightly spray large cookie sheet with cooking spray.

For bread: Combine flour, oats, sucanat with honey, yeast, cinnamon, and salt in food processor bowl; pulse machine on and off several times.

In small saucepan, heat water and oil until very warm, about 120 degrees.

With motor running, add liquids to flour mixture with egg white. Process until dough begins to form a ball; continue processing 1 minute.

Turn dough out onto a lightly floured surface. Knead apples into dough. Pat into 14-x-11-inch rectangle on cookie sheet. Let rise in a warm place for 40 minutes.

Heat oven to 400 degrees.

For topping: Combine oats, sucanat, cinnamon, and sour cream in a small bowl. Mix well. Spread evenly over top of dough; sprinkle with pecans or walnuts.

Bake for 20 minutes or until edges are golden brown. Let cool for 10 minutes. Cut and serve warm.

Ezekiel Bread
(FROM EZEKIEL 4:9)

This Ezekiel bread is the recipe that opened my eyes and birthed the vision of Daily Harvest. In my testimony, you will hear me speak of this bread and about how my interests were piqued when I discovered the goodness and benefits of eating stone-ground flour.

2½ cups hard red wheat berries
1½ cups spelt or rye
½ cup hulled barley
¼ cup millet
¼ cup lentils, preferably green
2 tbsp. great northern beans
2 tbsp. red kidney beans
2 tbsp. pinto beans
4 cups lukewarm water
1 cup honey
½ cup olive oil
2 tsp. salt
2 tbsp. yeast

In a large bowl, combine red wheat berries, spelt, hulled barley, millet, lentils, and beans. Mix well and grind in mill to make flour.

In a separate bowl, mix water, honey, and olive oil.

To the liquids, add freshly milled flour, salt, and yeast. Stir or knead until well mixed, about 10 minutes. This is a batter-type bread, and it will not form a smooth ball. Pour the dough into greased pans. You may use two large loaf pans, 10 x 5 x 3, or 3 medium loaf pans. Let dough rise in a warm place for 1 hour, or until the dough is almost to the top of the pan. Do not let it rise too much or it will overflow. Bake at 350 degrees for 45 to 50 minutes.

Note: This is a very sweet, moist, cakelike bread. You may also add fruits or nuts to this recipe. The combination of grains and beans makes this a complete-protein bread.

Cookies

Thinking back to the early days of baking in my garage, I remember Gale being the one who labored hours upon hours with the cookie recipes. Gale would bake a batch of cookies and my niece, Kay; her husband, Terry; my husband, Johnny; and I would perform a taste test. The men loved to perform this job, and they would trick Gale into baking more batches of cookies. Thank God, she's a patient person. I guess the early days of taste testing are the reason we bake such large cookies. Gale must have grown tired of feeding us so many cookies, so she decided to make them jumbo size.

Well, that has turned out to be a great thing; the customers at Daily Harvest Bakery & Deli just love the big ol' cookies we proudly display in our showcase. So if while you are baking these cookie recipes for your family and friends, they request that you bake the same recipe over and over, remember they are not requesting that you bake better, they are requesting you to bake more.

A Few Cookie Tips

The best way to cool cookies is on a wire rack until they become firm enough to handle.

Cookies should be stored in an airtight container or wrapped individually in plastic wrap.

The shelf life for Daily Harvest cookies is about 6 to 7 days.

Cookies in a Jar

Place your dry ingredients in a quart-size jar or bag. When you are ready to bake, just add the wet ingredients. These are great gift ideas.

Chocolate-Chip Cookie in a Jar

½ **cup sucanat**
½ **cup sucanat with honey**
1½ **cups stone-ground whole-wheat flour**
½ **tsp. baking soda**
½ **tsp. sea salt**
½ **cup semi-sweet chocolate chips**

M&M Cookie in a Jar

½ **cup sucanat**
½ **cup sucanat with honey**
1½ **cups stone-ground whole-wheat flour**
½ **tsp. baking soda**
½ **tsp. sea salt**
½ **cup M&Ms**

Oatmeal-Raisin Pecan Cookie in a Jar

Add the ingredients for this cookie recipe into the jar in layers.

LAYER 1:
½ **cup sucanat with honey**

LAYER 2:
½ **cup sucanat**

LAYER 3:
I **cup stone-ground whole-wheat flour**
½ **tsp. baking soda**
½ **tsp. baking powder**
¼ **tsp. sea salt**

LAYER 4:
I **cup rolled oats**

LAYER 5:
I **cup raisins**

LAYER 6:
½ **cup pecans**

To complete the jar recipes add the following:

½ **cup (I stick) butter, softened**
½ **tsp. vanilla**
I **egg**
Jar of dry ingredients

Cream together the butter, vanilla, and egg. Add the entire jar of dry ingredients. Mix well. Drop by spoonfuls onto cookie sheet. Bake at 350 degrees for 10 minutes, or until golden brown.

Yields: 15+ cookies

Chocolate-Haystack Cookie

1 cup freshly milled whole-wheat flour
½ tsp. baking soda
½ tsp. sea salt
½ cup cocoa powder
½ lb. butter
2 cups semi-sweet chocolate chips
6 eggs
2½ cups sucanat with honey
1½ tsp. vanilla
1 tbsp. almond extract
6 cups coconut

In a mixing bowl, combine flour, baking soda, salt, and cocoa. Set aside.

In a separate bowl, melt together butter and chocolate chips and set aside.

In a large bowl, combine eggs, sucanat with honey, vanilla, almond extract, and coconut. Add melted butter and chocolate chips. Mix in dry ingredients. Spoon onto greased baking tray.

Bake in a 350-degree oven for 12 to 15 minutes.

Yields: 1½ dozen cookies

Chewy Chocolate-Chip Cookie

1 cup sucanat
1 cup sucanat with honey
½ lb. butter
2 eggs
1 tsp. pure vanilla extract
½ tsp. water
3 cups stone-ground whole-wheat flour
1 tsp. baking soda
1 tsp. sea salt
1½ cups semi-sweet chocolate chips

Mix well the first six ingredients. Add the remaining three ingredients plus the chocolate chips. Spoon onto a greased cookie sheet. Press flat. Bake for 12 to 15 minutes in a 350-degree oven.

Yields: 12 large cookies

Oatmeal-Raisin Cookie

1 cup butter, softened
1 cup sucanat
1 cup sucanat with honey
2 eggs
1 tbsp. vanilla
2½ cups stone-ground whole-wheat flour
¼ tbsp. baking soda
½ tsp. baking powder
½ tsp. salt
2½ cups rolled oats
½ cup raisins

In a mixing bowl, cream together butter, sucanat, and sucanat with honey. Add eggs and vanilla and beat well.

Combine flour, baking soda, baking powder, and salt. Add to wet ingredients. Stir in rolled oats and raisins. Mix well. Scoop onto baking tray and bake for 12 minutes in a 350–degree oven.

Yields: 2 dozen cookies

Molasses Cookie

½ **lb. butter**
2 **eggs**
½ **cup molasses**
4 **cups freshly milled whole-wheat flour**
¼ **tbsp. sea salt**
¼ **heaping tbsp. cinnamon**
¼ **tbsp. ginger**
¼ **tsp. cloves**
2 **cups sucanat with honey**

Cream together butter, eggs, and molasses.

Combine flour, salt, cinnamon, ginger, and cloves and add to butter mixture. Mix well and refrigerate for 35 minutes. Pinch off a small amount of dough and roll into balls. Roll in sucanat with honey.

Bake at 350 degrees for 12 minutes.

Yields: 1 dozen cookies

No-Bake Peanut-Butter Rounds

2⅓ cups sucanat with honey
1 cup graham cracker crumbs
½ cup butter, unsalted
¾ cup peanut butter
10 oz. chocolate, semi-sweet chocolate chips or chocolate
   almond bark
2 tsp. vegetable oil
2 cups salted peanuts, finely chopped

Stir together the sucanat and graham cracker crumbs. Add the butter and peanut butter and work with your hands until thoroughly combined. Portion the dough into 30 1-inch balls and place on parchment paper.

Combine the chocolate and oil in a heatproof bowl. Melt the chocolate slowly.

Meanwhile, place the chopped peanuts in a shallow pan.

Dip the balls in the chocolate and roll in the peanuts. Place in a cool area so they will set.

White-Chocolate-Chunk Macadamia Cookies

¾ **cup sucanat**
½ **cup oatmeal**
⅓ **cup sucanat with honey**
1¾ **cups white wheat flour**
½ **tsp. baking soda**
½ **tsp. sea salt**
1 **cup butter**
2 **tbsp. honey**
1 **egg**
2 **tsp. vanilla**
8 **oz. white chocolate chips**
1½ **cups chopped macadamia nuts**

Place the sucanat, oatmeal, and sucanat with honey in the food processor. Process for 2 to 3 minutes. The oatmeal must be finely ground.

In a medium bowl, strain together the flour, baking soda, and salt.

With a mixer, in a large bowl, mix the butter and honey together on medium-low speed until smooth and creamy.

Add the oatmeal-sugar mixture. Add the egg and vanilla and beat for 1 minute. Add the white chocolate and macadamia nuts and mix until blended. Drop 1½-inch mounds of dough and place on baking sheet. Bake for 12 to 15 minutes at 350 degrees.

Yields: 2 dozen cookies, depending on size desired

M&M Cookie

1 cup sucanat
1 cup sucanat with honey
½ lb. butter
2 eggs
1 tsp. pure vanilla extract
½ tsp. water
3 cups stone-ground whole-wheat flour
1 tsp. baking soda
1 tsp. sea salt
1½ cups M&Ms

Mix well the first six ingredients. Add the remaining three ingredients. Spoon onto a greased cookie sheet. Top with a few M&Ms and press flat. Bake for 12 to 15 minutes at 350 degrees.
    Yields: 12 large cookies

Old-Fashioned Tea Cakes

1 stick butter, softened
2 cups sucanat with honey
2 tsp. vanilla
2 eggs
2½ cups stone-ground whole-wheat

Mix together the butter and sucanat with honey.

Add vanilla and eggs. Mix in flour. Batter should be a little stiff. Roll into balls and place on baking sheet. Press flat before baking. Bake for 12 to 15 minutes at 350 degrees.

Yields: 1-2 dozen cookies, depending on size desired

Oatmeal Cookie

1 cup butter, softened
1 cup sucanat
1 cup sucanat with honey
2 eggs
1 tbsp. vanilla
3 cups stone-ground whole-wheat flour
¼ tbsp. baking soda
½ tsp. baking powder
½ tsp. salt
2½ cups rolled oats

In a large bowl, cream butter, sucanat, and sucanat with honey. Add eggs and vanilla. Beat well.

In a separate bowl, combine flour, baking soda, baking powder, and salt. Add to butter-egg mixture. Stir in rolled oats and mix well. Scoop onto baking tray and bake for 12 minutes at 350 degrees.

Yields: 2 dozen cookies

Oatmeal-Raisin Pecan Cookie

I cup butter, softened
I cup sucanat
I cup sucanat with honey
2 eggs
I tbsp. vanilla
2½ cups stone-ground whole-wheat flour
¼ tbsp. baking soda
½ tsp. baking powder
½ tsp. salt
2½ cups rolled oats
½ cup raisins
½ cup chopped pecans

In a large bowl, cream butter, sucanat, and sucanat with honey. Add eggs and vanilla. Beat well.

In a separate bowl, combine flour, baking soda, baking powder, and salt. Add to butter-egg mixture. Stir in rolled oats, raisins, and pecans. Mix well. Scoop onto baking tray and top with a few sprinkles of pecans. Press in and bake for 12 minutes at 350 degrees.

Yields: 2 dozen cookies

Oatmeal Chocolate-Chip Cookie

I cup butter, softened
I cup sucanat
I cup sucanat with honey
2 eggs
I tbsp. vanilla
3 cups stone-ground whole-wheat flour
¼ tbsp. baking soda
½ tsp. baking powder
½ tsp. salt
2½ cups rolled oats
I cup semi-sweet chocolate chips

In a large bowl, cream butter, sucanat, and sucanat with honey. Add eggs and vanilla. Beat well.

In a separate bowl, combine flour, baking soda, baking powder, and salt. Add to butter-egg mixture. Stir in rolled oats and chocolate chips. Mix well. Scoop onto baking tray and bake for 12 minutes in a 350-degree oven.

Yields: 2 dozen cookies

Oatmeal Peanut-Butter Cookie

2 sticks butter, softened
1 cup sucanat
1 cup sucanat with honey
1 cup organic peanut butter
2 eggs
2 tsp. vanilla
2 cups milled whole-wheat flour
1 tsp. baking soda
1 tsp. sea salt
½ tsp. baking powder
1¼ cups rolled oats

In a large bowl, cream together the butter, sucanat, sucanat with honey, and peanut butter until smooth. Beat in the eggs and vanilla.

Combine the flour, baking soda, salt, and baking powder. Stir into the peanut-butter mixture. Mix in the oats. Mix well. Spoon onto a greased baking sheet. Bake at 350 degrees for 12 minutes.

Yields: 1-2 dozen cookies

Chocolate-Oatmeal Cookie

1 cup stone-ground whole-wheat flour
1/2 tsp. baking soda
1/2 tsp. sea salt
1/2 cup cocoa powder
1/2 lb. (2 sticks) butter
2 cups chocolate chips
6 eggs
2 1/2 cups sucanat with honey
1 1/2 tsp. vanilla
1 tbsp. almond extract
6 cups pressed oats

Combine in mixing bowl, flour, baking soda, sea salt, and cocoa. Melt butter and chocolate chips.

In a separate bowl, mix eggs, sucanat with honey, vanilla, almond extract, and pressed oats.

Add melted butter and chocolate chips into bowl with egg mixture and stir until well blended. Mix in dry ingredients. Spoon onto greased baking sheet. Bake in a 350-degree oven for 12 to 15 minutes.

Yields: 1 1/2 dozen cookies

Heath-Bar Cookie

1 cup sucanat
1 cup sucanat with honey
½ lb. butter
2 eggs
½ tbsp. pure vanilla extract
1½ tsp. water
3½ cups stone-ground whole-wheat flour
½ tbsp. baking soda
½ tbsp. sea salt
¾ cup chopped **Heath** candy bar

In a bowl, combine sucanat, sucanat with honey, butter, eggs, vanilla, and water. Mix well. Add flour, baking soda, and salt. Mix well.

Add chopped Heath pieces and mix. Spoon on to baking sheet. Sprinkle a few Heath pieces on top and press down. Bake in a 325-degree oven for 15 to 20 minutes.

Yields: 2 dozen cookies

Snickerdoodle

½ **lb. butter**
1½ **cups sucanat with honey**
2 **eggs**
½ **tbsp. vanilla extract**
2¾ **cups stone-ground whole-wheat flour**
½ **tbsp. cream of tartar**
1 **tsp. baking soda**
½ **tsp. sea salt**
¼ **cup sucanat with honey**
1 **tbsp. ground cinnamon**

Cream together butter, sucanat with honey, eggs, and vanilla. Blend in flour, cream of tartar, baking soda, and sea salt. Using large scoop, shape into balls.

Mix the ¼-cup sucanat with honey and cinnamon. Roll balls of dough in mixture. Place on baking sheet. Bake 8 to 10 minutes in a 350-degree oven.

No-Bake Cookie

I cup sucanat with honey
I cup milk
¼ cup cocoa powder
I tbsp. butter
2 cups peanut butter
4 cups oats

Bring the sucanat with honey, milk, cocoa, and butter to a rapid boil for 1 minute.

Add peanut butter and oats until thick. Drop on waxed paper. Work fast before the dough becomes too hard. Refrigerate for 30 minutes before serving.

Yields: 2 dozen cookies

Poppy-Seed Cookie

3 cups stone-ground whole-wheat flour
¼ tsp. sea salt
¼ cup poppy seeds
3 sticks, butter, unsalted and slightly firm
I cup sucanat with honey
3 large eggs yolks
I½ tsp. pure vanilla extract
Preserve filling of your choice, optional

Preheat oven to 350 degrees.

Mix together the flour, sea salt, and poppy seeds and set aside.

Place butter in mixer and beat until smooth. Pour in the sucanat with honey and mix. Add the egg yolks and vanilla, mixing only until blended. Using a wooden spoon, stir in the dry ingredients.

Note: Do not over mix this dough or it will become oily.

Roll the dough into balls about the size of large walnuts and place 2 inches apart on the cookie sheet. Using a wooden spoon with a rounded handle no wider than $1/2$ inch, make a deep indentation with the tip of the handle in the center of each cookie. If the dough sticks, dip the tip in flour for pressing.

Place the cookies in the oven. After 10 minutes, remove from the oven and repress each indentation. Then fill the centers with preserves. Do not over fill or preserves will run over.

Bake for an additional 4 to 5 minutes, or until golden brown around edges.

Yields: 5 dozen small cookies

Sugar Cookie

1 stick butter
1 cup sucanat with honey
1 egg
1¾ cup whole-wheat flour
1 tsp. baking powder
1 tbsp. milk
½ tsp. vanilla
¼ tsp. sea salt

Cream together butter and sucanat with honey. Add egg and mix. Add the remaining ingredients and mix until smooth. Refrigerate dough for 2 hours.

Place chilled dough onto a floured surface and roll out until it is $1/8$ inch thick. Cut with cookie cutter. Place on baking sheet and bake for 12 to 15 minutes in a 350-degree oven.

Yields: 2 dozen cookies

Nutty Fruit Bars

1 cup stone-ground whole-wheat flour
1 cup oats
⅔ cup sucanat with honey
2 tsp. baking soda
½ tsp. salt
½ tsp. cinnamon
⅔ cup buttermilk
3 tbsp. olive oil
2 egg whites, lightly beaten
1 apple, cored and diced
½ cup dried cranberries or raisins
¼ cup chopped nuts
2 tbsp. flaked coconut, optional

Preheat oven to 375 degrees.

Lightly oil 9-inch-square baking pan.

In a mixing bowl, combine flour, oats, sucanat with honey, baking soda, salt, and cinnamon. Blend. Add buttermilk, oil, and egg whites and beat with mixer until mixed well. Fold in fruits and nuts.

Spread mixture evenly in pan and top with a thin layer of coconut.

Bake for 20 to 25 minutes, or until cake tester comes out clean. Cool for 30 minutes and cut into bars.

Yields: 16 bars

Muffins and Pastries

Muffins

I think our muffins were what really got the wheels of Daily Harvest Bakery & Deli rolling. We started out with about three types of muffins on our menu. Today we proudly display a variety of about ten muffins. We sell them in our regular size, which is large, and we sell a mini muffin, which customers love to use for catering events. I think that at one time or another most every employee at Daily Harvest Bakery & Deli has baked muffins. If you ever visit us, be sure to ask Annette about her experience with baking muffins. It is quite a story.

James and Lynn Moore have been faithful customers of Daily Harvest Bakery & Deli since the beginning. Their favorite muffin is the Organic Seed muffin, but since we introduced Peaches-n-Cream, I think the competition is on. When the Moore's are in town, I visit with them while they eat breakfast at the bakery. We can always tell when James and Lynn are about to travel because one of the first items on their packing list is Daily Harvest muffins. Lynn will call and order two dozen muffins. They tell me they receive strange looks from security guards as their muffins convey through security check. Now that is what I would call a testimony.

I hope that as you bake these wonderful muffins for your friends, you will hear a story that will impress you as the Moore's have impressed us.

Basic Muffin Mix

This is our basic recipe, and we use it for all muffins. You can be as creative as you like with this recipe.

1 cup olive oil
2 cups sucanat with honey
4 eggs
4½ cups freshly milled hard-white whole-wheat flour
2 tbsp. sea salt
1½ cups skim milk
Fruits, optional
Nuts, optional

Preheat oven to 350 degrees.
Mix all ingredients. Fold in the fruits and nuts of your choice. Fill muffin tins level with batter. Bake for 20 to 25 minutes, or until toothpick comes out clean.
Yields: 12 medium muffins

Lemon Poppy-Seed Muffin

1 cup olive oil
2 cups sucanat with honey
4 eggs
4½ cups stone-ground whole-wheat flour
2 tsp. sea salt
1½ cups skim milk
1 tsp. lemon extract
3 tbsp. poppy seeds

Preheat oven to 350 degrees.

Mix all ingredients. Line muffin pan with liner, optional. Fill muffin tins level with batter. Bake for 20 to 25 minutes, or until toothpick comes out clean.

Yields: 12 medium muffins

Almond Poppy-Seed Muffin

1 tsp. almond extract
3 tbsp. poppy seeds
1 cup olive oil
2 cups sucanat with honey
4 eggs
4½ cups freshly milled hard-white whole-wheat flour
2 tsp. sea salt
1½ cups skim milk

Preheat oven to 350 degrees.

Mix all ingredients. Line muffin pan with liner, optional. Fill muffin tins level with batter. Bake for 20 to 25 minutes, or until toothpick comes out clean.

Yields: 12 medium muffins

Cinnamon Oat Muffin

2 tsp. cinnamon
2 cups oats
1 cup olive oil
2 cups sucanat with honey
4 eggs
4½ cups freshly milled hard-white whole-wheat flour
2 tsp. sea salt
1½ cups skim milk

Preheat oven to 350 degrees.

Mix all ingredients. Fill muffin tins level with batter. Bake for 20 to 25 minutes, or until toothpick comes out clean.

Yields: 12 medium muffins

Banana Nut Muffin

1 tsp. banana flavoring
1 cup olive oil
2 cups sucanat with honey
4 eggs
4½ cups freshly milled hard-white whole-wheat flour
2 tsp. sea salt
1½ cups skim milk
2 cups mashed bananas
2 cups chopped pecans

Preheat oven to 350 degrees.

Mix all ingredients, except bananas and pecans. Fold in the bananas and pecans. Fill muffin tins level with batter. Top each muffin with a pecan half. Bake for 20 to 25 minutes, or until tooth-pick comes out clean.

   Yields: 12 medium muffins

Cranberry-Apple Pecan Muffin

1 cup olive oil
2 cups sucanat with honey
4 eggs
4½ cups freshly milled hard-white whole-wheat flour
2 tsp. sea salt
1½ cups skim milk
1½ cups dried cranberries
1½ cups diced apples
1½ cups chopped pecans

   Preheat oven to 350 degrees.
   Combine olive oil, sucanat with honey, eggs, flour, salt, and skim milk. Mix well. Fold in fruits and nuts. Fill muffin tins level with batter. Top each muffin with a few pecan pieces. Bake for 20 to 25 minutes, or until toothpick comes out clean.
   Yields: 12 medium muffins

Blueberry Muffin

I cup olive oil
2 cups sucanat with honey
4 eggs
4½ cups freshly milled hard-white whole-wheat flour
2 tsp. sea salt
1½ cups skim milk
1½ cups blueberries, drained

Preheat oven to 350 degrees.
Combine all ingredients, except blueberries. Mix. Gently fold in blueberries. Fill muffin tins level with batter. Bake for 20 to 25 minutes, or until toothpick comes out clean.
Yields: 12 medium muffins

Blackberry Muffin

I cup olive oil
2 cups sucanat with honey
4 eggs
4½ cups freshly milled hard-white whole-wheat flour
2 tsp. sea salt
1½ cups skim milk
1½ cups blackberries

Preheat oven to 350 degrees.
Combine all ingredients, except blackberries. Mix. Gently fold in blackberries. Fill muffin tins level with batter. Bake for 20 to 25 minutes, or until toothpick comes out clean.
Yields: 12 medium muffins

Choc-o-Muffin

1 cup olive oil

2 cups sucanat with honey

4 eggs

4½ cups freshly milled hard-white whole-wheat flour

2 tsp. sea salt

1½ cups skim milk

¼ cup cocoa powder

½ cup miniature chocolate chips, semi-sweet or white
   chocolate

½ cup cream cheese icing*

Preheat oven to 350 degrees.

Combine olive oil, sucanat with honey, eggs, flour, salt, and milk. Mix well. Fold in cocoa and chocolate chips. Fill muffin tins level with batter. Add into each portion 1 tbsp. cream cheese icing. Bake for 20 to 25 minutes, or until toothpick comes out clean.

Yields: 12 medium muffins

*See recipe for cream cheese icing

Sweet Potato Muffin

1 cup olive oil
2 cups sucanat with honey
4 eggs
4½ cups freshly milled hard-white whole-wheat flour
2 tsp. sea salt
1½ cups skim milk
1 cup mashed sweet potato
½ cup pecans
¼ cup sucanat with honey

Preheat oven to 350 degrees.

Combine all ingredients, except sweet potato and pecans. Mix. Fold in sweet potato and pecans. Fill muffin tins level with batter. Sprinkle muffin tops with sucanat with honey. Bake for 20 to 25 minutes, or until toothpick comes out clean.

Yields: 12 medium muffins

Morning Glory Muffin

1 cup olive oil
2 cups sucanat with honey
4 eggs
4½ cups freshly milled hard-white whole-wheat flour
2 tsp. sea salt
1½ cups skim milk
¼ cup raisins
¼ cup pecans
¼ cup carrots
¼ cup pineapple

Preheat oven to 350 degrees.

Combine olive oil, sucanat with honey, eggs, flour, salt, and milk. Mix. Fold in the raisins, pecans, carrots, and pineapple. Fill muffin tins level with batter. Bake for 20 to 25 minutes, or until toothpick comes out clean.

Yields: 12 medium muffins

Organic Seed Muffin

1 cup olive oil
2 cups sucanat with honey
4 eggs
4½ cups freshly milled hard-white whole-wheat flour
2 tsp. sea salt
1½ cups skim milk
½ cup organic seed mixture*

Preheat oven to 350 degrees.

Combine olive oil, sucanat with honey, eggs, flour, salt, and milk. Mix. Fold in the seed mixture. Fill muffin tins level with batter. Bake for 20 to 25 minutes, or until toothpick comes out clean.

*Organic seed mixture: Combine equal parts organic pumpkin seeds, organic sunflower seeds, flax seeds, and sesame seeds.

Yields: 12 medium muffins

Strawberry-n-Cream Muffin

1 cup olive oil
2 cups sucanat with honey
4 eggs
4½ cups freshly milled hard-white whole-wheat flour
2 tsp. sea salt
1½ cups skim milk
1 cup fresh strawberries, quartered
½ cup cream cheese icing*

Preheat oven to 350 degrees.

Combine olive oil, sucanat with honey, eggs, flour, salt, and milk. Mix. Fold in strawberries. Fill muffin tins level with batter. Spoon 1 tbsp. cream cheese icing into each portion. Bake for 20 to 25 minutes, or until toothpick comes out clean.

Yields: 12 medium muffins

*See recipe for cream cheese icing

Peaches-n-Cream Muffin

1 cup olive oil
2 cups sucanat with honey
4 eggs
4½ cups freshly milled hard-white whole-wheat flour
2 tsp. sea salt
1½ cups skim milk
1 cup sliced peaches
½ cup cream cheese icing*

Preheat oven to 350 degrees.

Mix olive oil, sucanat with honey, eggs, flour, salt, and milk. Mix. Fold in peaches. Fill muffin tins level with batter. Spoon 1 tbsp. cream cheese icing into each portion. Bake for 20 to 25 minutes, or until toothpick comes out clean.

Yields: 12 medium muffins

*See recipe for cream cheese icing

Bacon and Cheese Muffin

2 cups freshly ground whole-wheat flour
2 tbsp. sucanat with honey
1 tbsp. baking powder
½ tsp. sea salt
1 large egg
⅓ cup melted butter
1 ¼ cups milk
2 tbsp. sour cream
10 slices of bacon, cooked crisp and crumbled
1 cup shredded cheddar cheese

Mix flour, sucanat with honey, baking powder, and salt.

Add egg, butter, milk, and sour cream. Stir until evenly moistened. The batter will be slightly lumpy. Fold in bacon and cheese. Do not over mix. Pour into muffin cups. Bake at 350 degrees until golden, about 25 minutes.

Yields: 12 to 15 medium muffins

Pastries

Whole-Wheat Cinnamon Roll

1 cup hot water
¼ cup olive oil
¼ cup honey
2½ cups stone-ground whole-wheat flour
1 tbsp. yeast
1½ tsp. salt
1 tbsp. dough enhancer, optional
¼ tsp. gluten
½ stick butter
1 cup cream cheese filling*
¼ cup cinnamon
¾ cup sucanat with honey
1-2 cups cream cheese icing**

Combine water, oil, and honey. Add ½ cup flour, yeast, salt, dough enhancer, and gluten. Mix thoroughly. Add the remaining flour and knead until smooth and elastic, about 10 minutes. Let rise in proofer until doubled in size. Punch down. Roll out on a floured surface into a large rectangular shape about ⅛ to ¼ inch thick. Spread on a thin layer of butter. Layer with cream cheese filling. Sprinkle with cinnamon and sucanat with honey. Roll into cylinder shape and cut in 1-inch strips. Place flat on pan lined with parchment paper. Press out with hand to flatten a little. Let rise until light and airy, about 25 to 30 minutes. Bake at 400 degrees for 20 to 30 minutes. Remove and ice with cream cheese icing.
   *See recipe for cream cheese filling
   **See recipe for cream cheese icing

Baked Turnover

1 lb. raw stone-ground whole-wheat dough*
¼ cup filling of your choice**
2 tbsp. butter, melted

Using 3 to 4 oz. of dough for each turnover, roll into a circle. The circles should be no more than ⅛ to ¼ inch thick. Fill with your choice of filling. Fold over and press edges together. Form a seal around the outside with a fork, pressing firmly all the way around the open part. Brush the top of each turnover lightly with butter. Place on a cookie sheet and bake for 20 to 25 minutes at 350 degrees.

*To make dough, see recipe for stone-ground whole-wheat bread.

**Fillings included in this book are: apple filling and blackberry filling. You can also use the following as fillings: chocolate pudding and banana pudding and coconut pie and lemon-cake pie mixtures.

Cream Cheese Danish

1 cup hot water
¼ cup olive oil
¼ cup honey
2½ cups stone-ground whole-wheat flour
1 tbsp. yeast
1½ tsp. salt
1 tbsp. dough enhancer, optional
¼ tsp. gluten
1 cup cream cheese filling*
1 cup cream cheese icing**

Combine water, oil, and honey. Add ½ cup flour, yeast, salt, dough enhancer, and gluten. Mix thoroughly. Add the remaining flour and knead until smooth and elastic, about 10 minutes. Let rise in proofer until doubled in size. Punch down. Roll into 4-oz. balls. Slightly flatten. Fill center with cream cheese filling. Place in pan lined with parchment paper. Let rise until light and airy. Bake at 400 degrees for 20 to 30 minutes. Remove and ice with cream cheese icing.

*See recipe for cream cheese filling
**See recipe for cream cheese icing

Raspberry Danish

1 cup hot water
¼ cup olive oil
¼ cup honey
2½ cups stone-ground whole-wheat flour
1 tbsp. yeast
1½ tsp. salt
1 tbsp. dough enhancer, optional
¼ tsp. gluten
1 cup cream cheese filling*
½ cup raspberry filling
1 cup cream cheese icing**

Combine water, oil, and honey. Add ½ cup flour, yeast, salt, dough enhancer, and gluten. Mix thoroughly. Add the remaining flour and knead until smooth and elastic, about 10 minutes. Let rise in proofer until doubled in size. Punch down. Roll into 4-oz. balls. Slightly flatten. Fill center with cream cheese filling. Place in pan lined with parchment paper. Let rise until light and airy. Bake at 400 degrees for 20 to 30 minutes. Remove and spread with raspberry filling. Complete by covering with cream cheese icing.

   *See recipe for cream cheese filling
   **See recipe for cream cheese icing

Kolache

4 American cheese slices
1 batch whole-wheat dough*
12 smoked link sausage

Cut each American cheese slice into 3 equal sections, about the same size as sausage. Set aside.

Place dough onto an oiled surface and roll into a rectangle, about ¼ inch thick. Cut into small squares, just a little bit larger than the sausage link. Place 1 sausage link and 1 cheese strip on each dough square. Roll up and seal at the seam by rolling on the table until the edge is sealed. Pinch and pull the ends in and do the same. This will keep the cheese from spilling out. Place on cookie sheet and bake for 20 minutes at 350 degrees. Let cool for 10 minutes and serve warm.

Yields: 12 kolache

*See recipe for stone-ground whole-wheat bread

Cakes

When we made our first stone-ground whole-wheat cake, I didn't know whether or not it would taste good. I knew we could bake very good muffins, cookies, and pastries. You would think that I would have learned not to second-guess whole-wheat products. After all, I have been in the business of grinding whole grains and baking healthy products for four years. When our first carrot cake came out of the oven, it filled the bakery with a take-me-back-to-my-grandmommie's-kitchen smell, and to my fellow bakers that fragrance was almost like heaven. There were two things my grandmommie loved to do—pray and fill her kitchen with the smell of baked goods. I know our cake recipes are somewhat simple, but aren't the simple things in life sometimes the best? So go ahead, pour yourself a tall glass of cold milk and prepare to create memories in your kitchen.

Rum Cake

2½ **cups stone-ground whole-wheat flour**
½ **tsp. baking powder**
¼ **tsp. sea salt**
¼ **cup sucanat with honey**
2 **cups sucanat**
½ **cup light butter, softened**
¼ **cup milk**
¼ **cup dark rum**
4 **large eggs**
½ **tbsp. vanilla extract**
½ **cup chopped pecans**

In a mixing bowl, combine all ingredients, except pecans, in their listed order. Beat at low speed for 1 minute. Increase speed to medium and beat for 2 minutes.

Grease and flour Bundt pan.

Sprinkle the batter evenly with pecans. Pour batter in prepared pan.

Bake at 350 degrees for 50 to 55 minutes, or until toothpick inserted in the center comes out clean.

Cool on wire rack for 15 minutes. Remove from pan and drizzle with hot rum glaze. Cool on wire racks for another 20 minutes before serving.

Hot Rum Glaze

1½ **cups sucanat with honey**
¾ **cup light butter**
¼ **cup light rum**

Mix all ingredients and bring to a boil in a saucepan. Boil for 3 minutes, or until thickened, stirring occasionally.

Carrot Cake

1½ cups stone-ground whole white-wheat flour
1 tsp. baking soda
½ tsp. sea salt
½ tbsp. ground cinnamon
3 eggs
½ cup sucanat
¾ cup sucanat with honey
⅛ cup oil
1¼ cups grated carrots
1 8oz.-can crushed pineapple in its own juice, do not drain
½ cup shredded frozen coconut, unsweetened
1½ cups finely chopped walnuts
1 recipe cream cheese frosting*

Preheat oven to 350 F.

Spray bottom and sides of 1 9-x-13-inch sheet cake pan.

Mix flour, baking soda, salt, and cinnamon in medium bowl.

In large bowl, beat eggs, sucanat, and sucanat with honey at medium speed for 1 to 3 minutes, or until thickened. Beat in oil at low speed. Stir in flour mixture until blended. Stir in carrots, pineapple, coconut, and 1 cup walnuts until blended. Pour into sheet cake pan. Bake 25 to 35 minutes, or until toothpick inserted in center comes out clean and cake pulls slightly away from sides of the pan.

Once cake has cooled, ice with cream cheese frosting.

Yields: 10 servings

*See recipe for cream cheese frosting

Cream Cheese Frosting

3 cups powdered sucanat with honey
6 oz. cream cheese, softened
½ cup butter, unsalted
1 tsp. vanilla extract
½ cups finely chopped walnuts, optional

To make powdered sucanat with honey, pulse in a food processor. Set aside

Beat cream cheese and butter in large bowl at medium speed for 3 minutes, or until well blended and smooth. Beat in vanilla. Add powdered sucanat with honey. Beat at low speed for 1 minute, or until well blended and smooth. Top with chopped walnuts.

Italian Cream Cake

¼ **lb. butter**
½ **cup olive oil**
2 cups sucanat with honey
5 eggs, separated
1 cup buttermilk
1 tsp. baking soda
2 cups white-wheat flour
1 tsp. vanilla
1 cup shredded coconut
½ **cup chopped nuts**
1 recipe cream cheese icing*

In a large mixing bowl, combine butter, olive oil, and sucanat with honey.

In a separate bowl, cream egg yolks, buttermilk, baking soda, flour, vanilla, coconut, and nuts. Add to butter mixture.

Beat egg whites until they become stiff. Fold into mixture.

Pour batter into a 9-x-13-inch greased sheet cake pan. Bake at 325 degrees for 30 minutes.

Once cake has cooled, ice with cream cheese icing.

*See recipe for cream cheese icing

German Chocolate Cake

4 oz. semi-sweet chocolate chips
½ cup boiling water
1 cup butter
1 cup honey
4 eggs, separated
1 tsp. vanilla
2 cups freshly milled flour, hard white
½ tsp. sea salt
1 tsp. baking soda
1 cup buttermilk
1 recipe coconut pecan frosting*

Melt chocolate in boiling water and cool.

Cream butter and honey. Beat in egg yolks. Stir in vanilla and chocolate. Set aside.

Mix flour, salt, and baking soda.

Add butter-chocolate mixture to the flour, alternating with buttermilk until mixed.

Beat egg whites until stiff. Fold into batter. Pour into 3 9-inch cake pans lined with wax paper. Bake at 350 degrees for 30 minutes. Remove from pans and let cool.

Once cake has cooled, ice with coconut pecan frosting.

*See recipe for coconut pecan frosting

Coconut Pecan Frosting

1 cup milk
¾ cup honey
3 egg yolks, beaten slightly
½ cup butter
1 tsp. vanilla
1 ⅓ cups fresh coconut
1 cup pecans

Cook and stir over medium heat until thickened milk, honey, egg yolks, butter, and vanilla. Color will change from light yellow to a very dark amber color. Let it boil for 10 minutes, or until it is as thick as it will get, but continue to stir! It will still seem a little runny, but it thickens as it cools. Add coconut and pecans. Spread when cool.

Cherry-Swirled Cheesecake

¼ **cup graham cracker crumbs**
21-oz. can of cherry pie filling
1 tsp. orange rind
16 oz. cream cheese
14 oz. low-fat sweetened condensed milk
4 egg whites
1 egg
⅓ **cup lemon juice**
1 tsp. vanilla
½ **cup sifted flour**

Preheat oven to 300 degrees.

Add graham cracker crumbs to bottom of a 9-inch cheesecake pan.

Purée cherry pie filling until smooth. Add orange rind and set aside.

In mixing bowl, beat cream cheese until fluffy. Gradually beat in condensed milk. Add egg whites, egg, lemon juice, and vanilla. Mix these well and add flour.

Pour ½ the batter in prepared 9-inch cheesecake pan. Spoon ½-cup cherry purée over the batter. Top with remaining cheesecake batter. Drop by spoonfuls the remaining cherry filling. With a knife, make swirls.

Bake for 60 minutes. Cool. Chill.

Yields: 12 servings

German Chocolate Cheesecake

1 cup chocolate graham cracker crumbs
2 tbsp. sucanat with honey
3 tbsp. melted butter
3 cups cream cheese, softened
¾ cup sucanat with honey
¼ cup cocoa
2 tsp. vanilla extract
3 large eggs
⅓ cup evaporated milk
⅓ cup sucanat with honey
¼ cup butter
1 large egg, lightly beaten
½ cup pecans
½ cup coconut

In a bowl, combine graham cracker crumbs, sucanat with honey, and melted butter. Press into the bottom of a 9-inch spring-form pan. Bake in a 325-degree oven for 5 minutes.

Combine cream cheese, sucanat with honey, cocoa, vanilla, and eggs. Pour over crust. Bake at 330 degrees for 35 minutes. Remove from oven, loosen cake from pan, and chill for 8 hours.

Meanwhile, combine in a saucepan evaporated milk, sucanat with honey, butter, and egg. Cook over medium heat, stirring constantly, for 7 minutes. Stir in pecans and coconut. Spread over cheesecake.

Yields: 12 servings

Pecan Autumn Cheesecake

3 cups graham cracker crumbs
9 tbsp. sucanat with honey
1½ tsp. ground cinnamon
1½ cups finely chopped pecans
¾ cup melted butter
48 oz. cream cheese, softened
1½ cups sucanat with honey
6 large eggs
1½ tsp. vanilla
8 cups thinly sliced apples
1 cup sucanat with honey
1½ tsp. cinnamon
¾ cup chopped pecans

Combine cracker crumbs, 9 tbsp. sucanat with honey, cinnamon, pecans, and melted butter. Press into the bottom of a 9-inch spring-form pan. Bake in a 350-degree oven for 10 minutes.

Combine cream cheese, 1½ cups sucanat with honey, eggs, and vanilla. Pour over crust and set aside.

To the apples, add 1 cup sucanat with honey, and cinnamon. Layer on top of the cream cheese mixture and top with pecans. Bake at 350 degrees for 1 hour and 10 minutes. Cool before removing from the pan.

Yields: 12 servings

Red Velvet Cheesecake

1½ cups chocolate graham cracker crumbs
¼ cup melted butter
1 tbsp. sucanat with honey
3 cups cream cheese, softened
1¼ cups sucanat with honey
4 large eggs, lightly beaten
3 tbsp. cocoa
1 cup sour cream
½ cup buttermilk
2 tsp. vanilla extract
1 tsp. white vinegar
2 oz. red food coloring
3 oz. cream cheese, softened
¼ cup butter, softened
2 cups powered sugar
1 tsp. vanilla extract
3 cherries

Combine graham cracker crumbs, melted butter, and 1 tbsp. sucanat with honey. Press into the bottom of a 9-inch spring-form pan. Set aside.

Mix the next nine ingredients. Pour batter onto crust and bake at 325 degrees for 10 minutes. Reduce heat to 300 and bake for 1 hour.

Cool cake for 30 minutes. Cover and chill for 8 hours.

Meanwhile, in a bowl, combine cream cheese, butter, sugar, and vanilla. Spread evenly over chilled cheesecake. Garnish with cherries.

Yields: 12 servings

Fresh Apple Cake

4 cups chopped Granny Smith apples
I cup sucanat with honey
I cup stone-ground whole-wheat flour
I tsp. baking soda
I tsp. ground cinnamon
½ tsp. sea salt
½ cup olive oil
2 eggs, beaten
2 tsp. vanilla extract
½ cup chopped walnuts*

Spray large Bundt pan with floured baking spray.

Mix together the apples and sucanat with honey. Mix in the flour, baking soda, cinnamon, and sea salt.

In a separate bowl, stir together oil, eggs, and vanilla. Add to this the apples and sucanat with honey. Mix well. Add walnuts. Pour into large Bundt pan. Bake for 45 minutes at 350 degrees.

Yields: 20 slices

*Optional: Add chopped walnuts to pan before pouring in batter.

Strawberry Cake

2 cups soft butter
8 eggs
4 cups sucanat with honey
2 tsp. vanilla extract
4½ cups whole-wheat flour
I tsp. salt
I heaping tbsp. baking soda
2 cups diced strawberries
I recipe cream cheese icing*

Mix all ingredients, except strawberries and icing. Fold in strawberries. Bake for 25 to 30 minutes in a 350-degree oven.

Once cake has cooled, top with cream cheese icing and garnish with a strawberry slice.

Yields: 10 slices

*See recipe for cream cheese icing

No-Bake Fruit Cake

4 cups graham cracker crumbs
I cup mixed candied fruit
I cup golden raisins
I cup chopped nuts
I cup miniature marshmallows
I can sweetened condensed milk

Line a 9-x-5 loaf pan with waxed paper.

Mix all the ingredients together until crumbs are thoroughly moistened. Pack into pan. Chill for 2 days.

This cake is especially popular at Christmas.

Eggnog Pound Cake

I lb. butter, softened
2 cups sucanat with honey
4 tsp. vanilla
8 eggs
3 cups stone-ground whole-wheat flour
3 tsp. baking powder
¾ tsp. salt
¾ tsp. nutmeg
I small box instant vanilla pudding mix
¾ cup oil
I½ cups eggnog

Cream butter, sucanat with honey, vanilla, and eggs. To this mixture, add remaining ingredients. Pour into Bundt pan and bake at 350 degrees for 30 minutes. Allow to cool in pan before removing from pan.

King Cake

2 lbs. dough
½ stick butter, softened
½ cup King Cake cream-cheese filling*
1 egg white, slightly beaten

Roll out dough into rectangle shape 30 x 18 inches.

Spread butter onto dough. Then spread cream cheese filling. Trim edges and bring them together. Brush top and ends with egg wash. Proof for 10 minutes and bake at 350 degrees for 30 minutes.

For fruit filled: Add fruit and sprinkle with ¼ cup sucanat with honey. Top with cream cheese icing and colored sprinkles.

This cake can be filled with any of the following: strawberries, blueberries, blackberries, or cinnamon.

*See recipe for King Cake cream-cheese filling

Note: At Daily Harvest, we bake this cake at Mardi Gras, Valentine, Easter, etc., changing the color of the sprinkles to match the season. For Mardi Gras, a baby is to be placed inside. For Easter, you could use a small cross, and for Valentine's, a heart. This cake is very tasty and can be used year-round with some creativity of your own.

King Cake Cream-Cheese Filling

8 oz. package cream cheese
1 cup sucanat with honey
2 tbsp. flour
1 tsp. vanilla
1 tsp. milk

Combine all ingredients and beat with mixer until smooth and creamy, about 10 minutes. This filling should be used while at room temperature to achieve a smooth consistency.

Cream Cheese Icing

6 oz. cream cheese, softened
½ cup butter, unsalted
3 cups sucanat with honey
1 tbsp. vanilla
½ cup honey or agave nectar

Mix all ingredients together and blend well.

Cream Cheese Filling

8 oz. package cream cheese
1 egg
½ cup sucanat with honey
½ tsp. vanilla
¼ tsp. salt

Mix all ingredients and whip until smooth.

Cupcakes

2 sticks butter
½ cup sucanat with honey
1 tsp. vanilla
2 eggs
1 cup white wheat flour
1 tsp. baking powder
⅛ tsp. sea salt
½ cup milk

Beat butter, sucanat with honey, and vanilla until creamy. Add eggs and mix well. Add dry ingredients and milk and mix well. Pour into individual muffins liners. Bake for 20 minutes at 325 degrees.
Yields: 12 cupcakes

Whole-Wheat Brownies

3 eggs
1½ cups sucanat with honey
¾ tbsp. vanilla
1½ sticks butter
1½ cups semi-sweet chocolate chips
¾ cup stone-ground whole-wheat flour
½ tsp. salt
1 cup chopped pecans

Mix eggs, sucanat with honey, and vanilla. Set aside.
Melt butter and chocolate chips. Add to egg mixture. Add flour and salt and mix. Fold in pecans. Bake for 30 minutes at 350 degrees.
Yields: 13 x 9 pan

Pies and Puddings

Pies

The pies are probably the newest product on our catering menu. I wanted to add pies because it was my favorite holiday dessert. And I guess it is human nature to want people to experience the things that you like. Since we had a large family, my mama would begin baking a week before Christmas. However, at Daily Harvest, we make a commitment to bake fresh everyday.

I have converted some of my mama's old recipes by incorporating stone-ground whole-wheat and sucanat sweetener. If, when baking our pie-filling recipe, you want the filling to be lighter, just add a little light cool whip. Although this is not the pie we would eat while sitting around my granddaddy's old piano singing Christmas hymns, it still makes a mighty fine pie.

Stone-Ground Whole-Wheat Pie Crust

2 sticks butter
2½ cups stone-ground whole-wheat flour
1 tsp. sea salt
1 tsp. sucanat with honey
3-6 tbsp. ice water

Cut sticks of butter into ½-inch cubes and place in freezer for 15 minutes.

Combine flour, sea salt, and sucanat with honey in food processor and pulse to mix. Add butter until mixture resembles coarse meal. Add ice water. When you can pinch crumbly dough and it holds together, the dough is ready. If the dough doesn't hold together, add a little more water and pulse again.

Remove dough from machine and place in a mound on a clean, slightly floured surface. Gently shape into 2 discs. Roll out until large enough to cover inside of pie pan. Place into pie pan and bake for 15 minutes at 350 degrees before pouring in pie filling.

Yields: 2 pie crusts

Apple Filling

This recipe can be used for a pie filling or to fill baked turnovers.

2 tbsp. butter
4 Granny Smith apples, peeled, cored, and diced
½ cup sucanat with honey
1½ tsp. cinnamon
1 tsp. lemon juice

Melt butter in pan. Add diced apples, sucanat with honey, cinnamon, and lemon juice. Cook over medium heat for 15 minutes, or until the apples are soft. Pour into pie shell or use to fill turnovers*.

To make pie, pour filling into pie shell and bake for 10 to 15 minutes. Cut and serve after pie has cooled completely.

*See recipe for baked turnover

Blackberry Pie Filling

4 cups blackberries, fresh or frozen
1 cup sucanat with honey
⅔ cup whole-wheat flour
2 tbsp. cornstarch

If using frozen blackberries, thaw.

Combine sucanat with honey, flour, and cornstarch in a pan. Add blackberries. Cook and stir over medium heat until thick. Pour into pie shell or use to fill turnovers.

To make pie, pour filling into pie shell and bake for 10 to 15 minutes. Cut and serve after pie has cooled completely.

Yields: 4 turnovers

*See recipe for baked turnover

Buttermilk Pecan Pie

½ cup butter
2 cups sucanat with honey
2 tsp. vanilla extract
3 eggs
3 tbsp. stone-ground whole-wheat flour
¼ tsp. salt
I cup buttermilk
¾ cup chopped pecans
I 9-inch stone-ground whole-wheat pie crust*, unbaked

Preheat oven to 425 degrees.

Cream butter and sucanat with honey, adding one at a time. Stir in vanilla and 3 eggs, adding one at a time.

Combine flour and salt and slowly stir into creamed mixture. Add buttermilk and combine well.

Sprinkle pecans into bottom of 9-inch whole-wheat pie shell. Pour buttermilk mixture on top and bake for 90 minutes. Cool before slicing.

Yields: 8 servings

*See recipe for stone-ground whole-wheat pie crust

Coconut Pie

2 cups sucanat with honey
¾ cup stone-ground whole-wheat flour
1 cup evaporated milk
3 eggs, separated
2 cups boiling water
⅛ tsp. salt, small pinch
½ tsp. vanilla
1 stick butter
2 cups fresh ground coconut
1 9-inch stone-ground whole-wheat pie crust*

In a saucepan, cook sucanat with honey, flour, milk, egg yolks, water, and salt on high heat for 3 minutes. Then cook on medium heat until mixture begins to bubble. Add vanilla and butter, and coconut. Stir and let sit until warm, not cold. Pour into pie shell and cool in refrigerator for 3 minutes.

*See recipe for stone-ground whole-wheat pie crust

Daily Harvest Mud Pie

½ cup butter
1 cup stone-ground whole-wheat flour
¼ cup pecans, chopped
8 oz. cream cheese
1 cup sucanat with honey
1 cup Cool Whip®
2½ cups Daily Harvest chocolate pudding*
2½ cups instant vanilla pudding
Chocolate shavings, garnish

For crust, mix butter, flour, and pecans and press into 9-x-13-inch pan. Bake for 20 minutes at 350 degrees.

For filling, combine cream cheese, sucanat with honey, and $1/2$ cup Cool Whip®. Spread into crust. Layer chocolate pudding, then vanilla pudding on top of cream cheese layer. Top with rest of Cool Whip®. Sprinkle on chocolate shavings.

Yields: 1 pie

*See recipe for chocolate pudding

Note: Instant pudding may be substituted for Daily Harvest chocolate pudding.

Chocolate Pie

1 batch chocolate pudding*, warm
1 stone-ground whole-wheat pie crust**

Pour warm chocolate pudding into whole-wheat pie shell and cool in refrigerator for at least 30 minutes.

Yields: 8 servings

*See recipe for chocolate pudding

**See recipe for stone-ground whole-wheat pie crust

Lemon Cake Pie

1 stone-ground whole-wheat pie crust*
1 cup sucanat with honey
¼ cup freshly ground whole-wheat flour
¼ cup butter, melted
⅛ tsp. sea salt
2 large eggs, separated
1 large lemon, juiced
1 cup low-fat milk

Preheat oven to 350 degrees.

Bake pie shell for 5 minutes. Set aside to cool.

In a large bowl, combine sucanat with honey, flour, butter, sea salt, and egg yolks. Beat until smooth. Add lemon juice. Beat slowly while adding milk.

In another bowl, beat egg whites until stiff. Fold into lemon mixture. Pour into pie shell and bake for 40 minutes, or until center is set. Allow pie to cool for 10 to 15 minutes before slicing.

Yields: 8 servings

*See recipe for stone-ground whole-wheat pie crust

Puddings

Chocolate Pudding

This chocolate pudding recipe belongs to my mama (Odeal Smith), and I can remember her making this pudding for special occasions and holidays.

2 cups sucanat with honey
¾ cup stone-ground whole-wheat flour
4 tbsp. cocoa
I cup evaporated milk
3 eggs, separated
2 cups boiling water
⅛ tsp. salt, small pinch
½ tsp. vanilla
I stick butter

Cook sucanat with honey, flour, cocoa, milk, egg yolks, water, and salt on high heat for 3 minutes. Then cook on medium heat until the mixture begins to bubble. Add vanilla and butter. Stir and let sit until warm, not cold. As a pudding, it can be served warm or cool.

Banana Pudding

2 cups sucanat with honey
½ cup stone-ground whole-wheat flour
1 can evaporated milk
3 eggs
2 cups boiling water
⅛ tsp. salt, small pinch
½ tsp. vanilla
1 stick butter
20-25 vanilla wafers
3 bananas, cut into slices

Cook first six ingredients on high heat for 3 minutes. Then cook on medium heat until mixture begins to bubble. Add vanilla and butter. Stir and let sit until warm, not cold.

Place wafers and banana slices into bottom of a dish. Pour warm mixture over cookies and bananas, making 2 layers. Pudding may be served warm or cold.

Yields: 10 servings

Daily Harvest Bread Pudding

5 slices stone-ground whole-wheat bread, crumbled fine
1 cup sucanat with honey
¼ tbsp. baking powder
¼ tbsp. cinnamon
⅛ tbsp. nutmeg
¼ can evaporated milk
⅓ cup milk
¼ cup butter
2 eggs
2 tbsp. vanilla

RUM SAUCE:
⅓ cup sucanat with honey
¼ cup light butter
⅛ cup light rum

Using a food processor, crumble bread slices. Mix all dry ingredients. Set aside.

Mix all wet ingredients.

Combine wet and dry mixtures. Pour into small baking dish sprayed with non-stick spray. Bake for 25 minutes in a 350-degree oven.

For rum sauce: Combine sucanat with honey, butter, and rum. Pour over hot bread pudding.

Yields: 8 servings

Casseroles

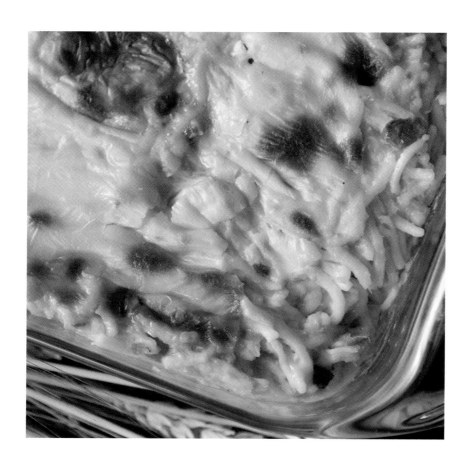

I think the first casserole we baked at Daily Harvest was the sweet potato casserole. It was our first holiday season, and we didn't have any idea what we were in for. It was great that people loved us and allowed us to do their holiday cooking, but we were very inexperienced and unprepared for what we were about to experience.

It was the day before Thanksgiving, and we were already behind! We had lost count of the number of ordered sweet potato casseroles, and I had to beg my husband, Johnny, to help us. I asked him, "How many sweet potato casseroles do I have left to bake?" He replied, "Don't look up, just keep on prepping sweet potatoes." I had never worked in a commercial kitchen, so I didn't know all the back-of-the-house slang. I said to Gale and the bakers, "Y'all, let's hurry because we are in the woods." Gale laughed at me and replied, "Teresa, it's not in the woods, it's in the weeds." Weeds or woods, it didn't matter, all I knew was that we were not keeping up with the orders.

We made it through our first holiday, and we sure did learn a lot. The next year we were more prepared for the long list of casseroles.

Breakfast Casserole

24 eggs
3 tbsp. butter
I cup diced onions
I cup shredded cheddar cheese
½ cup diced bell pepper
½ cup bacon pieces, bacon bits
I tsp. salt
I tsp. cornstarch

Combine all ingredients. Pour into a 13-x-9 baking dish well coated with cooking spray or oil. This casserole can also be baked in a muffin pan for individual servings. Bake for 30 to 35 minutes in baking dish, or 15 to 20 minutes in muffin pan. Salt and pepper to taste.

Yields: 12 servings

Sweet Potato Casserole

3 cups sweet potato, mashed
I cup sucanat with honey
2 eggs
I tbsp. vanilla
½ cup melted butter
½ cup shredded coconut

TOPPING:
½ cup sucanat
½ cup stone-ground whole-wheat flour
⅓ cup butter, softened
I cup chopped pecans

Mix the sweet potato, sucanat with honey, eggs, vanilla, butter, and coconut. Pour into a buttered baking dish. Bake for 20 minutes in a 350-degree oven.

For the topping: Mix all ingredients together and crumble over the casserole. Bake an additional 20 minutes at 350 degrees.

Yields: 10-15 servings, depending on portion size

Green Bean Casserole

2 tbsp. onion
2 tbsp. butter
I tsp. salt
I tsp. pepper
I tsp. sucanat with honey
2 tbsp. flour
I cup sour cream
2 20-oz. cans green beans
8 oz. mozzarella cheese, low-moisture or fresh
Bacon, crushed

Sauté onions in butter for 5 minutes. Add salt, pepper, sucanat with honey, and flour. Now add sour cream and let melt. Set aside for topping.

Place green beans in casserole dish. Top with mozzarella cheese. Let bake in a 350-degree oven until cheese melts, about 10 minutes. Remove from oven and pour mixture over beans. Return to oven and bake another 10 minutes. Top with crushed bacon and bake 5 minutes longer.

Yields: 10-15 servings, depending on portion size

Cornbread Dressing

CORNBREAD:
2 cups freshly ground yellow corn meal
I cup stone-ground whole-wheat flour
I ½ cups milk
2 tbsp. baking powder
½ tsp. sea salt
5 ¼ cup oil

DRESSING:
2 sticks butter, melted
½ cup chopped onions
½ cup bell pepper
½ cup chopped celery
I ½ cups evaporated milk
3 cups chicken broth
2 slices whole-wheat bread, crumbled
3 eggs
I tbsp. salt
I tsp. pepper

To make the cornbread, combine all ingredients and mix well. Pour into greased baking dish and bake for 30 minutes in a 325-degree oven.

Allow to cool and crumble into mixing bowl. Set aside.

In a pan, melt butter. Add onions, bell pepper, and celery. Sauté for 10 minutes.

Pour vegetables over cornbread and add milk, broth, crumbled wheat bread, eggs, salt, and pepper. Mix well.

Pour into greased baking dish and bake for 35 minutes, or until golden brown, at 375 degrees.

Yields: 10-15 servings, depending on portion size

Simply Corn Casserole

3 lb. bag of whole-kernel corn
2 cups cream cheese
1 cup chopped onions
¾ cup chopped bell peppers
½ can evaporated milk
½ tsp. salt
½ tsp. pepper

Combine all ingredients and mix well. Cook on stovetop for 20 minutes.

Yields: 10 servings

Quick and Easy Chicken Tetrazzini

This makes a very nice casserole dish, and it's quick and easy.

2-4 chicken breasts, bone in
8-9 oz. dry spaghetti
1 cup chicken broth
1 10-oz. can cream of mushroom soup
1 10-oz. can cream of chicken soup
1 10-oz. can Rotel® diced tomatoes
1 cup sour cream
½ cup shredded cheddar cheese

Boil chicken breast until cooked through. Remove chicken, reserving liquid. Set aside and let cool.

Boil the spaghetti in the broth from the cooked chicken. Drain and add to casserole dish.

Meanwhile, debone chicken and cut into bite-size pieces.

To the spaghetti, add the remaining ingredients. Combine. Mix in chicken. Top with shredded cheese and bake for 20 to 30 minutes, or until browned on top.

Yields: 10-15 servings, depending on portion size

Chicken and Cheese Enchiladas

4-5 chicken breast, deboned and grilled
2-3 tbsp. water
1½ cups shredded cheddar cheese
1½ cups shredded pepper jack cheese
2 cups enchilada sauce
10 whole-wheat tortillas

Place grilled chicken breast on a cookie sheet. Add water and cover with foil. Bake for 20 minutes at 350 degrees.

Slice chicken into thin strips, cutting diagonally across each piece. Mix well with 1 cup of the cheeses and 1 cup sauce. Place a generous amount of mixture, about ½ cup, onto tortillas. Roll the tortillas, folding the ends in to enclose the chicken mixture.

Place ½ cup sauce in the bottom of 2 baking pans. Add 5 enchiladas to each pan. Cover with ½ cup sauce and cheese. Cover and bake for 20 minutes in a 350-degree oven. Remove cover and bake for an additional 10 minutes.

Yields: 10 servings

Chicken and Spaghetti

4-5 chicken breasts, bone in
1 tbsp. salt
3 cups water
8 oz. dry spaghetti
1 cup chopped onions
1 cup chopped bell pepper
2 6-oz. cans mushrooms
1 tbsp. minced garlic
1 30-oz. can spaghetti sauce
Parmesan cheese, to taste

In a pot, boil chicken in 3 cups of salted water until cooked through. Remove from pot, reserving liquid. Set aside and cool.

Boil pasta in liquid from cooked chicken, according to package directions. Drain, reserving broth, and set aside.

Meanwhile, debone chicken breasts.

Sauté onions, bell pepper, mushrooms, and garlic. Add spaghetti sauce. Cook for 15 minutes. Add chicken breasts. Add cooked noodles.

Pour in to large deep-dish baking dish. Add more broth if mixture is too dry. Sprinkle with Parmesan cheese and bake for 15 minutes in a 350-degree oven.

Yields: 10-15 servings, depending on portion size

Baked Chicken Breast

4 chicken breasts
I tsp. salt
½ tsp. pepper
½ tsp. garlic
I tsp. Tony Chachere's Creole Seasoning®
Butter
2 cups chicken broth
I cup cream of mushroom soup
I cup cream of chicken soup

Lightly sprinkle both sides of chicken breasts with seasonings. Place in baking dish and top with butter.

Pour chicken broth over chicken and bake, covered for 2 hours, in a 350-degree oven.

Combine cream of mushroom soup and cream of chicken soup and pour into the juices in the pan.

Place back in the oven and bake uncovered until browned.

Yields: 10-15 servings, depending on portion size

Wraps, Salads, and More

This section of the book was birthed through many, many sleep-less nights and a lot of new ideas. First, let me make this dis-claimer: The nights without sleep were not a great concern of mine because I was at home snug in my bed, sleeping like a baby. Teresa was the one burning her candle at both ends. She is like the Energizer Bunny®, but I need my eight to twelve hours of sleep each night.

Teresa functions just fine on a wink or two, and in between each wink, the wheels turn over new ideas she can present to me the next day. There have been occasions when the next day did not come soon enough for her, and after she had waited as long as she could, I would receive a 3:00 A.M. wake-up call. I would sleepily answer the phone, and on the other end of the line would be a very excited Teresa. Now there was a time when if my phone rang after midnight, I would be alarmed and dread to answer it, but since we opened the bakery, I have become accustomed to early morning calls. It goes something like this: *Ring, ring.* I sleepily look at my phone, squinting and straining to read the number and the time. This never works because I can't see very well that early in the morning, especially after being jolted from my deep slumber. Phone in hand I slowly and sleepily say, "Hello." On the other end comes the exclamation, "Hey, Gale, I've been thinking and . . ." "Hello," is usually all I get to say until she has allowed her idea to burst into my ear, ending with, "So, what do you think?" Smiling, I knew another new idea had been born during the night, and when I got to work at my usual time, which is ten minutes after I should have been there, I would get to sample a new product.

As you browse through this section of the cookbook, I hope you will appreciate the many nights Teresa has deprived herself (and me) of some much needed sleep. I also hope you will try each one, understanding that they were birthed with you in mind, and enjoy the fruit of our labor from Daily Harvest.

Gale Green

Breakfast Wrap

This wrap is good any time of the day or night, and it is quick and easy.

1 tbsp. butter
6 eggs
¼ cup diced bell pepper
¼ cup diced onions
½ cup shredded cheddar cheese
¼ cup salsa
6 ham slices
6 whole-wheat tortillas
¼ cup chopped jalapeños, optional

Place butter in skillet and allow to melt.

Beat eggs together and pour into skillet. Allow eggs to begin to cook. Mix in bell pepper and onions and scramble. When eggs are completely cooked, mix in cheese and salsa.

Place 1 slice of ham on each tortilla. Top with a generous amount of egg mixture. At this time, you can add jalapeños and more cheese if you would like. Fold the ends of the tortilla shell in and begin to roll into a cylinder shape. Place on a panini grill or griddle to brown the shell. Use any left over salsa for dipping.

Yields: 6 wraps

Tomato-Basil Wrap

This wrap can be served hot or cold. Cut in half and share with a friend for lunch with a good bowl of soup and some great conversation.

¼ **cup Vidalia onion dressing**
4 tomato-basil tortillas
I cup mixed greens or lettuce
I cup mozzarella cheese
8 tomato slices
I tbsp. sun-dried tomatoes
I tsp. dried basil

Spread a layer of Vidalia onion dressing on each tomato-basil tortilla. Add mixed greens. Top greens with a layer of mozzarella cheese, 2 tomatoes, and sun-dried tomatoes. Sprinkle with basil.

Fold in end of each shell and roll into a cylinder-shaped wrap. Place on panini grill or toast in hot skillet.

Yields: 4 wraps

Tomato-Basil 4-Cheese Wrap

Use the recipe above and add to it three more types of cheese and a few roasted pecan pieces. Be flexible with the amount. Go light or be very generous. It's your call . . . just enjoy.

Cheddar cheese
Parmesan cheese
Goat cheese

Grilled Chicken Wrap

2 boneless chicken breasts, grilled
1 tsp. rosemary and garlic seasoning
½ cup Vidalia onion dressing
4 whole-wheat tortillas
½-¾ cup mixed greens
1 tsp. sun-dried tomatoes
¼ cup cheddar cheese
¼ cup mozzarella cheese
1 tsp. goat cheese, optional
3-4 jalapeño slices, optional

Grill chicken and cut into diagonal strips. Thin strips make a better wrap. Sprinkle with the seasoning and coat well. Set aside.

Spread a layer of Vidalia onion dressing on tortillas. Top with greens, sun-dried tomatoes, chicken, cheeses, and jalapeños. Fold in ends and roll into a cylinder-shaped wrap. Place on panini grill or grill in skillet. Grill long enough to heat wrap through and to melt cheese. Cut in half and serve hot.

Yields: 4 wraps

Cranberry-Pecan Crisps

1 loaf cranberry pecan bread*, sliced
½ cup butter, melted
½ cup sucanat with honey

Diagonally cut each slice of bread. You will have 4 pizza-shaped wedges from each slice of bread. Place in a large bowl. Gradually pour in melted butter and toss to evenly coat. Sprinkle in sucanat with honey and toss again until evenly coated. Layer onto cookie sheet and bake for 10 minutes in a 350-degree oven. Remove from oven and stir. Bake for another 5 minutes, or until golden brown and crisp.

*See recipe for cranberry pecan bread

Daily Harvest Croutons

10-12 bread slices
¼ cup butter, melted
1 tbsp. onion powder
1 tbsp. garlic powder
1 tbsp. rosemary garlic
⅛ tsp. parsley
⅛ tsp. Italian seasoning
⅛ tsp. salt
⅛ tsp. pepper

Cut bread into 1-inch cubes. Drizzle with melted butter. Sprinkle with seasonings and toss until evenly coated. Bake at 350 degrees until toasted. Cool. Store in Ziploc® bag until needed.

Daily Harvest Chicken Salad

TOP SECRET RECIPE

When we opened Daily Harvest, we only baked breads, muffins, and cinnamon rolls. It had never crossed my mind to serve sandwiches. However, when we opened the sandwich station, people loved the combination of good fresh stone-ground breads with homemade tuna salad, sliced turkey, sliced ham, and sliced roast beef, but their all-time-favorite sandwich was and still is our Daily Harvest chicken salad.

When we first began making our chicken salad, we made about two quarts at a time and only sold it in sandwiches. Now we make our chicken salad in five-gallon containers and sell it by the pound. Customers keep their refrigerators stocked with Daily Harvest chicken salad for late-night sandwiches and/or to serve with wheat crackers for their personal catering events. Our chicken salad has been a big contribution to the popularity of Daily Harvest Bakery & Deli. I hope y'all will understand why we are keeping the recipe a secret. Our employees are sworn to secrecy. Ok, Annette and Cortez are suckers for flattery, but don't try to tempt them with sweet comments, it just might work!

Cool Summer Pasta Salad

8 oz. dry pasta
4 broccoli tops
4 cauliflower tops
½ cup shredded carrots
2 tbsp. butter
½ cup sliced green and/or black olives
1 cup chicken, cubed, optional
2 cups Italian dressing

Boil pasta for 15 minutes. Drain.

Chop broccoli and cauliflower. Sauté broccoli, cauliflower, and carrots in butter for 5 minutes.

In a large bowl, combine the remaining ingredients, pasta, and vegetables and mix well.

Low-Fat Fruit Salad

This recipe was featured on KTVE Channel 10, the NBC affiliate in Monroe, Louisiana, during the month of August 2007.

DRESSING:
8 oz. pineapple low-fat yogurt
6 oz. pineapple juice
1 tsp. poppy seeds

SALAD:
12 oz. pineapple cubes
2½ cups sliced strawberries
2 medium apples, cut into bite-size pieces
2 cups greens

In a bowl, mix yogurt, pineapple juice, and poppy seeds. Set aside.

In a separate bowl, add greens and top with fruit. Drizzle with dressing.

Creamy Fruit Salad

Quick, easy, healthy . . . does it get any better?

1 small box sugar-free vanilla pudding
3 cups strawberries, sliced
3 cups grapes
2 cups pineapple, diced
3 bananas, sliced
2-3 cups fruit juice of your choice

Prepare vanilla pudding according to package directions.
Mix all ingredients and chill for 30 minutes.
Yields: 15-20 servings

Fruit Pizza

1 batch sugar cookie dough*
16 oz. cream cheese
⅔ cup sucanat with honey
1 tsp. vanilla flavoring
2 tbsp. cornstarch
1 cup fresh-squeezed orange juice
2 cups sliced strawberries
1 can sliced peaches
2 bananas, sliced
2 kiwi, sliced

Spread sugar cookie dough onto a pizza pan. Bake in a 350-degree oven for 12 to 15 minutes. Allow to cool.

Combine cream cheese, $^1/_3$ cup sucanat with honey, and vanilla. Mix well and spread over cool crust.

Cook remaining sucanat with honey, cornstarch, and orange juice in microwave or on stovetop until thickened.

Slice fruit and place on top of cream cheese layer. Pour orange-juice syrup over fruit and chill in refrigerator until ready to serve.

Yields: 10 servings

*See recipe for sugar cookie

Yoggi

This is good any time of the day, but we sell a lot of these as a breakfast item. It is tasty and filling.

½ cup Daily Harvest yogurt*
¼ cup fruit, blueberries, bananas, or strawberries
¼ cup Daily Harvest granola**

In a small dish, place 1 to 2 scoops daily harvest yogurt. Top with fruit of your choice and Daily Harvest granola.

*Any prepared yogurt may be substituted for Daily Harvest yogurt.

**See recipe for Daily Harvest granola

Daily Harvest Granola

2 sticks butter
1 tbsp. cinnamon
1 cup honey or agave nectar
8 cups rolled oats
2 cups pecan halves
2 cups walnuts, chopped
1½ cups pumpkins seeds
1½ cups sunflower seeds
1½ cups raisins
1½ cups dried cranberry

Boil butter, cinnamon, and honey/agave nectar for 3 minutes. Pour over oats and stir well to coat. Add nuts and seeds. Bake at 350 degrees for 10 minutes. Remove from oven and stir. Bake 5 more minutes, or until golden brown. Add fruit and stir.

This is the base of this recipe. Try other ingredients to create your own personal touch. This can be a fun and creative recipe.

Yields: 15 12-oz. bags

Daily Harvest Granola Bar

1 ⅓ cup butter
1 cup sucanat
1 cup sucanat with honey
2 eggs
2 tsp. vanilla
1 tsp. baking soda
1 tsp. sea salt
3 cups stone-ground whole-wheat flour
4 cups Daily Harvest granola*

Preheat oven to 375 degrees.
Spray baking pan with nonstick spray.
Mix all ingredients together and spread onto a cookie sheet. Bake until brown for 20 to 25 minutes. Cut into bars.
*See recipe for Daily Harvest granola

Almond Joy Granola

½ **lb. butter**
1 cup honey or agave
1 tbsp. cinnamon
8 cups rolled oats
4 cups shredded coconut
2 cups whole almonds
2 cups melted almond bark bar

Bring butter, honey or agave, and cinnamon to a boil and boil for 3 minutes, or until it begins to thicken.

Combine rolled oats, coconut, and almonds. Spread onto cookie sheet. Pour syrup over mix and bake for 10 minutes in a 375-degree oven. Remove from oven and stir. Bake for an additional 10 minutes, or until golden brown. Let cool for 20 to 30 minutes and add chocolate.

Yields: 10 bars

Daily Harvest Peanut-Butter Granola Bar

⅓ **cup butter**
⅔ **cup peanut butter**
½ **cup sucanat**
½ **cup sucanat with honey**
I **egg**
I **tsp. vanilla**
½ **tsp. baking soda**
½ **tsp. sea salt**
I **cup stone-ground whole-wheat flour**
2 **cups Daily Harvest granola***
¼ **cup organic oats**
½ **cup melted almond bark bar**

Preheat oven to 375 degrees.
Spray cookie sheet with nonstick spray.

Mix all ingredients and spread onto cookie sheet. Bake until light brown, about 20 to 25 minutes. Cut into bars. This recipe should make one cookie sheet.

Yields: 10 bars

*See recipe for Daily Harvest granola

Mama's Cream

This is an old-home recipe. My mama, Odeal Smith, would make this for my brother and me when we were small. Mama would make me sit on top of the old ice-cream churn while my brother, Rickey, would turn the crank. It was hard work, but our mouths would water as we waited for the cream to make.

My mama loved sharing this ice cream at family gatherings, at church functions, or any other occasion she thought needed the comfort of her "good ol'" ice cream. Good memories go well with this ice cream and are almost as good.

2 cups sugar*
2 cans PET® evaporated milk
I can sweetened condensed milk
I tsp. vanilla
4 cups whole milk**
I dash of salt

Place all ingredients in the cylinder of your ice-cream maker. Set your timer for 40 minutes, or until the ol' hand crank is too hard to turn. Wait for the finished product.

*We substitute sucanat with honey.

**May substitute skim or low-fat milk.

Drinks

Juice Hut

We opened the juice hut about a year after we opened Daily Harvest. While at a bakery expo in Chicago, Gale and I attended a bakery show everyday, examining new baking equipment, products, and ways to package our products. Though I enjoyed the show, I really didn't see anything new I wanted to take home. Feeling a little disappointed, we shifted our focus to shopping of a different sort.

We were staying in a hotel on the Magnificent Mile, and as you know, the shopping there is great. Being two Southern women who love to shop, we walked the streets around our hotel everyday. During our walks, I noticed a juice bar on almost every corner. On their menus were drinks such as fresh-squeezed orange juice, fresh-squeezed carrot juice, and fresh-squeezed apple juice. I was drinking fresh squeezed juice, and I loved it. A light bulb clicked on in my head, and an idea was born.

Six months passed and my idea had become a reality. We added a new sign inside Daily Harvest that read "Juice Hut." Our customers were happy to watch fresh fruits and vegetables being squeezed right before their eyes, chilled, and placed in their hands within minutes, accomplished without adding any white sugar or artificial flavorings.

To make your own healthy, great-tasting juices at home, I suggest you purchase a juicer. You can buy them at most department stores. You will feel the difference. Fresh raw fruit is a natural cleanser and fresh raw vegetables are natural healers. And the biggest plus of all is IT TASTES GREAT!

Wheatgrass Juice

Wheatgrass is possibly the most nutritious item on Juice Hut's menu. Wheatgrass juice is the juice extracted from the red wheatberry seed sprouts. This strain of wheat has been used for thousands of years all around the world for its healing properties. Wheatgrass juice pulls unwanted toxins out of the body and replaces them with beneficial vitamins and minerals, has only ten to fifteen calories per teaspoon, and includes all eight essential amino acids. One ounce of fresh wheatgrass contains the vitamin, mineral, and enzyme equivalent of two pounds of green vegetables.

Since in it's natural form, wheatgrass is very fibrous and cannot be broken down in the digestive tract of humans, it must be liquefied before it can be utilized. In this state, it is considered to be a complete food, which can assist in fighting a range of chronic ailments. The medical benefits of wheatgrass juice include the following: purifying the blood and liver, improving digestion and the body's ability to heal wounds, increasing hemoglobin production, and preventing tooth decay.

Individuals can grow their own wheatgrass, and to begin you will need about 1 cup of some type of wheat berry. At Daily Harvest, we use the red wheat berry. The berry needs to be soaked in clean tap water for about 24 hours before planting. Plant the berry in an organic potting soil and keep in a dark room until it begins to break through the soil. When you see the growth, water and set in a sunny area. Allow to grow for about 5 days. It should reach a height of 6 inches before you cut for juicing.

The juicing process requires a wheatgrass juicer. It extracts the moisture from the grass. It should be taken in 1 to 2 ounce shots about 4 times a week. Because of its strong detoxifying effects, it is important to go easy when first taking wheatgrass juice. One ounce a day is a good place to start.

Orange Berry Smoothie

8 oz. Daily Harvest fresh-squeezed orange juice*
4 oz. blueberries, fresh
4 oz. strawberries
4 oz. raspberries
6 oz. Daily Harvest gelato yogurt**
10 oz. crushed ice

Place all ingredients, except ice, in a high-speed blender. Blend for 15 seconds. Add ice and blend for 60 seconds.

*May substitute your own fresh-squeezed orange juice or any prepared fresh orange juice.

**May substitute any prepared yogurt.

Yields: 12 oz.

Straw-nana Smoothie

1 banana
6-8 strawberries, fresh
10 oz. crushed ice

Place banana and strawberries in a high-speed blender. Blend for 15 seconds. Add ice and blend for 60 seconds.

Yields: 12 oz.

Ban-apple Smoothie

I Red Delicious apple, whole
I banana
10 oz. ice

Place apple and banana in a high-speed blender. Blend for 15 seconds. Add ice and blend for 60 seconds.
Yields: 12 oz.

Blue Bayou Smoothie

I banana, whole
4 oz. blueberries, fresh
I tbsp. liquid sucanat with honey, optional
10 oz. ice

Place all ingredients, except ice, in a high-speed blender. Blend for 15 seconds. Add ice and blend for 60 seconds.
Yields: 12 oz.

Old-Fashioned Cherry Nectar

The words "cherry nectar" are words that could always put a smile on the faces of my brother, Rickey, and me. It meant two things: One, that my cousins from Monroe were coming to visit, and two, that we were going to go to Hodge Advance Drug Store to get cherry nectar.

Even though we were poor, when my Aunt Dorothy and Uncle

Purvis and their two kids, Pat and Ronald, would come to visit us, my mama would somehow find money to buy Rickey and me cherry nectar from the drug store. Before Mrs. Thelma could take our orders, we were screaming CHERRY NECTAR! My mouth would water as I watched that reddish-pink liquid make foam as it surrounded the vanilla ice cream. I tried to drink it slow so it would last longer, but I was so carried away by the atmosphere of the soda fountain and sweet flavors rushing down my throat that before long I could hear that slurping sound coming from my frosty glass. I used to hear my daddy preach about heaven's streets of gold and walls of jasper. But I would imagine heaven having a huge drug store with gold bar stools and all the free cherry nectars a little girl could drink.

Today, I get to make cherry nectars for my customers. My employees and I make good and tasty cherry nectars, but I assure you, we can't make them as well as Mrs. Thelma Harville could. Enjoy!

2 scoops vanilla gelato or yogurt
6 oz. cherry nectar soda
Whipped cream, garnish
I cherry, garnish

Place gelato in 12-oz. glass. Pour chilled cherry nectar soda over the top. Garnish with whipped cream and a cherry.

Tropical Root Beer Float

2 scoops coconut gelato
12 oz. root beer

Add gelato to a 16-oz. tumbler. Pour chilled root beer over and enjoy.

Yields: 12 oz.

Iced Latte Java Punch

2 shots espresso
2 cups hot water
2½ cups sucanat with honey
1 quart vanilla gelato
1 quart chocolate gelato
Vanilla, to taste
Nutmeg, to taste
Cinnamon, to taste

Mix espresso, water, and sucanat with honey until sucanat melts. Chill thoroughly. Fold in gelato. Add vanilla, nutmeg, and cinnamon to taste.

Yields: 12 oz.

Chocolate Pecan Delight Latte

1 cup milk
2 shots espresso

12 OZ. LATTE:
1 shot chocolate sauce
¼ shot praline syrup
¼ shot walnut syrup
¼ shot caramel syrup

16 OZ. LATTE:
1½ shots chocolate sauce
½ shot praline syrup
½ shot walnut syrup
½ shot caramel syrup

20 OZ. LATTE:
1½ shots chocolate sauce
¾ shot praline syrup
¾ shot walnut syrup
¾ shot caramel syrup

Heat and froth 1 cup milk.

To espresso, add the appropriate amounts of flavors, depending on size of drink. Pour in milk.

Chocolate Turtle Latte

1 cup milk
2 shots espresso

12 oz. LATTE:
1½ shots chocolate sauce
½ shot caramel syrup
½ shot praline syrup

16 oz. LATTE:
1½ shots chocolate sauce

1 shot caramel syrup
1 shot praline syrup

20 oz. LATTE:
1½ shots chocolate sauce
1½ shots caramel syrup
1½ shots praline syrup

Heat and froth 1 cup milk.

To espresso, add the appropriate amounts of flavors, depending on size of drink. Pour in milk.

Cinnamon Roll Latte

1 cup milk
2 shots espresso

12 oz. LATTE:
1 shot caramel syrup
1 shot cinnamon syrup

16 oz. LATTE:
1½ shots caramel syrup
1½ shots cinnamon syrup

20 oz. LATTE:
2 shots caramel syrup
2 shots cinnamon syrup

Heat and froth 1 cup milk.

To espresso, add the appropriate amounts of flavors, depending on size of drink. Pour in milk.

Gingersnap White Mocha Latte

1 cup milk
2 shots espresso

---

12 oz. Latte:
1 shot white chocolate sauce
1 shot ginger spice syrup

16 oz. Latte:
1½ shots white chocolate sauce
1½ shots ginger spice syrup

20 oz. Latte:
2 shots white chocolate sauce
2 shots ginger spice syrup

Heat and froth 1 cup milk.

To espresso, add the appropriate amounts of flavors, depending on size of drink. Pour in milk.

Heath Toffee Latte

1 cup milk
2 shots espresso

---

12 oz. Latte:
1½ shots chocolate sauce
1 shot English toffee syrup

16 oz. Latte:
2 shots chocolate sauce
1½ shots English toffee syrup

20 oz. Latte:
2½ shots chocolate sauce
2 shots English toffee syrup

Heat and froth 1 cup milk.

To espresso, add the appropriate amounts of flavors, depending on size of drink. Pour in milk.

Milky Way Latte

1 cup milk
2 shots espresso

12 OZ. LATTE:
1½ shots caramel sauce
1½ shots chocolate sauce

16 OZ. LATTE:
2 shots caramel sauce
2 shots chocolate sauce

20 OZ. LATTE:
2½ shots caramel sauce
2½ shots chocolate sauce

Heat and froth 1 cup milk.

To espresso, add the appropriate amounts of flavors, depending on size of drink. Pour in milk.

Peppermint Patty Latte

1 cup milk
2 shots espresso

12 OZ. LATTE:
1 shot chocolate sauce
½ shot peppermint syrup

16 OZ. LATTE:
1½ shots chocolate sauce
1 shot peppermint syrup

20 OZ. LATTE:
2 shots chocolate sauce
1½ shots peppermint syrup

Heat and froth 1 cup milk.

To espresso, add the appropriate amounts of flavors, depending on size of drink. Pour in milk.

Pumpkin Spice Frappe

FRAPPE BASE:
2 tbsp. cinnamon
1 tsp. nutmeg
16 oz. Torani Pumpkin Spice
  syrup

8 OZ. FRAPPE:
1 tbsp. cinnamon
½ tsp. nutmeg

16 OZ. FRAPPE :
1 scoop vanilla latte mix
1 scoop of ice

To make frappe base, combine cinnamon, nutmeg, and Torani Pumpkin Spice syrup.

To make 8 oz. frappe, measure 8 oz. frappe base. Add cinnamon and nutmeg. Blend.

To make a 16 oz. frappe, measure 4 oz. frappe base into blender with vanilla latte mix and ice. Blend on #4 setting.

Appendix A

The Benefits of Whole Wheat
by Teresa Gordon

People are more concerned about their health today than ever before, and with good reason. Doctors' offices and hospitals stay full with sick people. We all ask ourselves the question, "What can we do to enhance our health?" I believe one way is through whole grains.

To gain a good understanding of how whole grains can be beneficial to our health, we need to learn what whole grains are. For instance, whole-wheat flour, brown rice, barley, and oatmeal are all considered whole-grain foods. Whole grains include all three parts of a grain kernel—the bran, germ, and endosperm.

Whole-grain wheat contains powerful antioxidants that may help prevent cancer, diabetes, and heart disease. Over the years, researchers have said fiber was the key to wheat's disease-fighting power. Now, it's believed that the antioxidants in whole grain also play a major role. Antioxidants can be found in vitamins E and D, but researchers say eating whole grains is critical for the antioxidants to be absorbed.

An article in the November 2002 issue of *Harvard Heart Letter* states, "Americans can be healthier eating the right kind of carbohydrates." For eons, humans have eaten diets based on whole grains. Whole grains provide fiber, healthy fats, vitamins, minerals, and plant enzymes. However, most of the grain our population consumes is refined wheat. White flour looks very "pure" and makes bread and pastries fluffy, but important nutrients are lost in the process because the bran and germ are stripped away. Highly processed carbohydrates, such as those found in white flour and white rice, give a quick burst of blood sugar followed by a sharp rise in insulin. High levels of both glucose and insulin increase the chances of developing diabetes and heart disease.

Chances of developing these diseases can be decreased by introducing whole grains into our diet. Whole grains bring slower, steadier increases in blood sugar and insulin. According to the Harvard-based Nurses' Health Study, women and men who ate two to three servings of whole-grain products each day were thirty percent less likely to have a heart attack or die from heart disease over a ten-year period than women and men who ate less than one serving per week. This study also showed that men and women who rarely ate whole grains were more likely to develop Type II diabetes compared with those who ate two to three servings per day.

Over the past few years, researchers have begun to look closely at how the quality of carbohydrates affects general health and specifically, the role whole grains can play in promoting health. According to goals set by the U.S. Government, called "Healthy People 2010," at least three of the recommended six servings per day of grain products should be whole grain.

Appendix B

Selected Baker's Terms

Dough Enhancer: This product makes a softer bread and helps it to have a longer shelf life.

Sea Salt: This is salt that has been derived from seawater and dried by solar power. You can substitute it teaspoon for teaspoon for regular table salt in any recipe. If you do not have sea salt, use plain table salt.

Stone-ground whole-wheat flour: We have a stone mill at Daily Harvest by which we grind our flour daily to achieve the most valuable source of vitamins and minerals possible. If you do not have access to a mill, you may purchase flour from us daily or purchase your own mill.

Sucanat or **Sucanat with Honey:** These products are organic sweeteners derived from the first squeezing of the sugar cane. Then it is immediately dried to form hard crystals. Sucanat is used to replace brown sugar in recipes, and sucanat with honey is substituted for white refined sugar. Use sucanat to replace any recipe calling for white refined sugar, cup for cup.

Wheat Gluten: This product is made through a detailed process achieved by washing and rinsing a mass of dough to cleanse away starch. This process leaves a concentrated mass of high protein, which is dried and ground into a fine powder.

Visit our web site at www.dailyharvestbakery.com to purchase most of your baking needs, such as the ones listed above. Feel free to e-mail us at dailyharvest@comcast.net.

Index